The Equal Opportunities Book

A guide to employment practice in voluntary organisations and community groups

By Jim Read

InterChange Books

First published in 1988 by InterChange Books, 15 Wilkin Street, London NW5 3NG. 01-267 9421.

2

THE
EQUAL
OPPORTUNITIES
BOOK

READ, JIM
    The equal opportunities book; a guide to employment practice in voluntary organisations.
    1. Great Britain. Voluntary organisations.
    Personnel. Employment. Equality of opportunity.
    I. Title
    331.1'33

    ISBN 0-948309-08-3
                Copies available from InterChange. Please send payment with order, plus 60p (P+P).
                Trade distribution by Turnaround Distribution, 27 Horsell Road, London N5 1XL. 01-609 7836.

The Author
Jim Read currently works as a counsellor, freelance writer and trainer on mental health issues. His written work has appeared in several publications including *The Guardian, New Society, Social Work Today, Voluntary Action, City Limits, Community Care, Peace News* and *Open Mind.*
In the past he has worked for the Greater London Citizens Advice Bureaux Service, Friends of the Earth, the National Council for Voluntary Organisations and City and Hackney Association for Mental Health. He has also been a shop steward for the Association of Clerical, Technical and Supervisory Staffs.

InterChange
Based in Kentish Town, North London, InterChange is a community centre in the widest sense; providing a comprehensive range of projects, services and facilities, it exists to stimulate greater community involvement and activity.
As a registered charity we run community arts and education projects, including the Weekend Arts College and the Log Cabins, with soft adventure play for the Under Fives. The multi media resource centre gives low cost access to expensive audio-visual, printing and computing technology. InterChange's organisation development team provide advice, training and consultancy on all aspects of running community organisations.

InterChange Books
InterChange Books are aimed at helping groups and individuals to organise themselves effectively and achieve their own objectives. Drawing on InterChange's wide experience of community work, InterChange Books are practical and clearly written handbooks which demystify and make accessible areas such as the law, publishing and printing.

Contents

3

4

THE
EQUAL
OPPORTUNITIES
BOOK

Foreword

This book describes why equal opportunities is an important issue for all voluntary organisations which employ staff. It shows how women, people from ethnic communities, people with disabilities, lesbians and gay men, and working class people are often treated unfairly by employers. It explains how to draw up an Equal Opportunities policy for your organisation and how it can be put into practice. Details of relevant legislation are given; showing the ways employers are obliged to treat their workers and potential workers fairly, the opportunities it offers to compensate for past injustice and also the limitations it imposes on organisations which would like to go further than the law permits. In addition there are many suggestions for action which can be taken without having to consider the legal position.

What the book does not do is include a 'model' Equal Opportunities policy for your organisation to copy, or a list of instructions to follow. Adopting a policy and making it work requires thought, debate and commitment. This can best be achieved by members of the management committee and employees taking the time to decide what they think about these issues, what they want their organisation to achieve and what is the best way to do it. To try and bypass that process may result in a policy which looks good on paper, but it is unlikely to be effective in practice.

This guide offers the facts, the theory and the encouragement which will make it easier for the people in your organisation to take constructive action towards it becoming a genuine equal opportunities employer. Its intention is not to make it possible to avoid the discussion and work which is needed to achieve that goal, but to provide the information which will encourage that process.

Acknowledgements

I have received practical help and support for this project from numerous people. Without them it would not have seen the light of day. I have particularly come to appreciate the work of the Commission for Racial Equality, the Equal Opportunities Commission and the National Council for Civil Liberties. Cathy Itzen and the members of her writers' support group have given me consistent encouragement. I would especially like to thank Fiona Adamson, Patrick Blundy, Julia Phillips and Desrie Thomson for their thorough criticisms and suggestions for improvements, and Alison Clixby for her editing and enthusiasm.

I do, of course, have no-one to blame but myself for any inaccuracies or inadequacies in the text.

Introduction

The British people are divided from each other by class, race, sex, disability, age, sexuality and religious belief. Often the segregation is physical: people live in different parts of town according to class status; families move in search of work and leave elder relatives behind; people with disabilities are prevented from taking part in many activities because of lack of proper facilities; many Black people are trapped in decaying inner city areas by economic circumstances. Most women work only with other women. They might have their homes with men but be separated from them by their perceptions of a world which treats them very differently. Lesbians and gay men may mix with heterosexual women and men but find it unsafe to talk to them about their experience of life. Some get a raw deal, facing prejudice, hostility and economic discrimination, while others enjoy privileges and have an easier time. All suffer from the restricted outlook, the isolation, and the feelings of not belonging that such division causes.   A purpose of many voluntary organisations is to try and alleviate the worst effects of this unhappy state of affairs. 'Voluntary Organisation' is a term which covers a broad range of groups. Some are small, informal and employ no paid staff. Others have been established many years, have a national constituency and command budgets of millions of pounds. What they tend to have in common is a desire to somehow 'make things better', whether it be for their own members, a local community or the entire planet.

Whatever the primary purpose of a voluntary organisation, it can make a contribution towards breaking down these painful divisions by examining its own policies and practices and changing them, to make them fair to all and to compensate for past discrimination. This should

9

cover every aspect of its work, from the way it conducts its meetings, to the recruitment of staff, the design of its publicity material and the services it offers members and clients. This is what is meant by an Equal Opportunities Policy, or more correctly, an Equal Opportunities Policy and Programme (EOPP) – because a policy without a programme to put it into effect will not achieve anything.

EOPPs are increasingly being adopted by employing organisations, including large public companies and local authorities. They are encouraged by such bodies as the Commission for Racial Equality and the Equal Opportunities Commission. (See Useful Organisations at the back of this book.) Voluntary organisations have been at the forefront in developing EOPPs, the impetus often coming from staff, through their union sections. The informal and flexible management style to be found in many voluntary organisations, combined with a commitment to social change, encourages them to take initiatives in this area. There can be an additional incentive to adopt an EOPP. Some local authorities are insisting that organisations to whom they give grants must demonstrate that they have EOPPs. But for every voluntary organisation which has an EOPP, there are many more which have not yet given any consideration to the issue or have token and ineffective policies.

It is hoped that this guide will encourage those which have not yet considered this policy area to do so. It brings together information and ideas from a wide variety of sources with the intention of making it easier for organisations to develop their own EOPPs, which reflect their unique situations. The guide offers no blueprints.

The emphasis here is very much on EOPPs as they affect the employment of staff. Employment is a particularly important aspect of an Equal Opportunities policy because of its economic implications. All discrimination has an economic element to it and for any group being treated unfairly, employment is a major issue. This particularly applies in an era in which paid work is in short supply.

There is a variety of legislation which must be taken into account when considering action on equal opportunities. It particularly applies to employment issues and is often baffling to people trying to work out what action they can take, to compensate for past mistreatment experienced by groups such as Black people and women. (For a definition of Black see page 44). The need to clarify the legal situation is a further reason for focusing on employment practice.

This is a practical guide, with the emphasis on what can be done and how to do it. However equal opportunities is a policy area which stirs up strong feelings: feelings of hopefulness, excitement and interest, but also of anger, guilt and confusion. It is important to acknowledge these feelings. It is when they are not acknowledged that bad feelings are likely to cause the reader to 'retire hurt', with a headache, halfway through the guide.

The use of language is often an issue about which disputes occur. For instance, you may have been involved in an argument about whether to use 'chairman', 'chairperson' or 'chair'. The position taken here is that language evolves with the times. We should not be slaves to outmoded useage which causes confusion or reinforces prejudice. Words like 'man', 'he' or 'him', when used to refer to men or women, do reinforce assumptions that men are more important than women. It is worth using the odd inelegant phrase to avoid this.

Another problem area is how to refer to various groups which experience oppression. Often the words used reflect the condescending attitudes or mistaken beliefs that others have about them.

An example of condescending language is calling women 'girls'. This implies that women are less mature than men. Because young people are less respected than adults in this society, it also implies that women are less deserving of respect than are men.

Some people who have been diagnosed as mentally ill (including the author), claim that there is no such thing as 'mental illness'. They were, or are, suffering from emotional distress, often caused by the difficulties of living in an oppressive society. To talk about equal opportunities for the mentally ill, is then to start from a mistaken position, or at least one which will cause offence to some of those whose rights the policy is supposed to be recognising.

A principle used in this book is to choose the language most favoured by those it is used to describe. It will not satisfy everybody. There is not always consensus. Not everyone who has been labelled 'mentally ill' rejects the diagnosis, and not everyone who rejects 'mental illness' is satisfied with 'mental distress', which is used here. The debate should and will continue and eventually something better will emerge as part of the wider discussions about equal opportunities.

The exact meaning of some words is not always clear. What do we mean by 'ethnic community' or 'sexism'? Dictionaries do not always help. When such words are used here the meaning they are intended to have is given. But elsewhere they may be used in a slightly different way.

We have a choice. We can use disputes about language as a way of attacking, or scoring points off each other, or as the starting point for intelligent debate.

The author's basic motivation for writing this guide stems from his own realisation of the part that class discrimination and irrational attitudes to mental health have played in shaping his employment opportunities. Anyone involved in thinking about and taking action on the issues raised in this book would do well to start by considering their own position in society; and considering what they have to gain – in real human terms – from ending discrimination, even if it means losing some privileges.

Why an Equal Opportunities policy?

Just imagine...
- Most MPs are women.
- The majority of students at Cambridge and Oxford Universities are from working class backgrounds.
- Black women and men are on the boards of large companies.
- The Prime Minister is openly gay.
- You are served in a shop by someone in a wheelchair.
- Your organisation's annual conference is truly representative of its constituency.

Until all this is possible, there is not equality of opportunity.

The current position is that it is easier to get a job, easier to get a well-paid job and easier to occupy a position of power and authority if, by accident of birth, you are white or upper class, or male, than if you are not. Groups which are disadvantaged in this respect include women, people from ethnic communities, working class people, lesbians and gay men, and people with disabilities. Between them they make up the vast majority of the population. Many people, of course, have to deal with the multiple disadvantage of being in several of these groups.

The mistreatment of people in this way, which comes from the way society is organised, is usually called oppression. The oppression of women is called sexism, the oppression of Black people, racism etc. Much of this oppression arises from lack of awareness rather than deliberate intention. It has psychological and economic components. For people with physical disabilities, a psychological component for their oppression (often referred to as 'able-bodeism') is the way they are frequently treated as if they cannot think for themselves. An economic component arises from them being excluded from many jobs that they could do as well as anyone, if employers thought about their needs.

Oppression is sometimes described as prejudice plus power. People in a position to oppress others are able to do so because they have power over them. Men may be prejudiced against women and women against men, but because men hold more power they are able to mistreat women in a systematic way. An example of men's prejudice against women is thinking that women do not make good managers. When a male-dominated board of directors fails to appoint women to managerial positions because of this prejudice, their behaviour is oppressive to women.

**TOWARDS
LIBERATION**

The roots of oppression lie deep in the psychological and political history of the human race. What matters here, is how it is perpetuated and how this process can be challenged and overcome, for the liberation of all people.

No one is born with oppressive attitudes towards other people, but as we grow up we are bombarded with oppressive images: books where everyone lives in a cosy heterosexual family and is able-bodied; racist jokes, TV programmes where men fight and women stand around looking impressed.

Young people are dependent on adults for information about how the world is, and trust them. What is more, adults have the power over young people to force their oppressive attitudes on to them, with the threat of physical violence or the withdrawal of love or approval, if they resist. The relationship between adults and young people in this society therefore itself involves oppression.

On a blatant level a white child may be forbidden to play with a Black child. More subtly, a boy is more likely than a girl to be stopped from crying; setting the scene for him later, as an adult, to complain that his wife is 'over-emotional' and send her off to the doctor. Eventually under the pressure of misinformation and intimidation, young people find it too difficult and painful to hang on to what they know to be true – that all people are good and equal. It becomes buried, to a lesser or greater extent, under a layer of acquired oppressive attitudes that are in turn, passed on to the next generation. In a similar way, victims of oppression start to believe what they hear about themselves: they are stupid , worthless, undeserving, and so on.

Although all this may sound heavy and depressing, there are grounds for optimism. If we have to be coerced into being racist or sexist etc. in the first place, then surely it must be possible to free ourselves of these attitudes.

It is worth stating that oppression is often perpetuated in

subtle ways, by people who are not aware that they are doing it and may be shocked or offended if it is pointed out. In an oppressive society, unless you are actively countering the oppression you are perpetuating it. There is no neutral ground. A voluntary organisation may 'welcome everyone to its ranks'. But if it holds its annual conference in a venue which is not wheelchair accessible, and does not offer to provide a sign language interpreter for deaf people , it is unintentionally excluding people with certain disabilities from its activities. Similarly, an agency which offers an advice service in an area where the first language of many of the residents is Bengali, but does not have a Bengali speaker on its staff, is not providing equal access to its services.

Voluntary organisations hold positions of power in society. They have money and are able to influence events. (Though both funds and degree of influence may fall far short of what they want.) They can offer work and may offer services to the community.

If their power is to be channelled in the direction of liberation from all forms of oppression, voluntary organisations may have to make fundamental changes in their policies and the way they operate. Changes in the organisation need to be accompanied by changes in the attitudes of the people who work for, or otherwise represent it. These two components of change are inseparable. For example, a decision may be made to try and recruit more Black workers by advertising in the ethnic community press. It is more likely to bring results if the white members of the interviewing panel have attended training sessions to make them more aware of how unconscious value judgements may cause them to unintentionally discriminate against Black candidates. Heterosexual staff are more likely to think about dealing with their prejudices agains lesbians and gay men, if the organisation includes in its EOPP Statement of Intent, a commitment to treat people equally, regardless of how they define their sexuality.

Changing attitudes requires training. Changing practices requires hard information – about the law, about the recommendations of bodies such as the Equal Opportunities Commission (See Useful Organisations at the back of this book) and about the experience of other voluntary organisations. The main purpose of this guide is to provide this information, but there is more about training in Chapter Two.

Formulating and implementing a policy and programme

An organisation intending to offer genuine equality of opportunity needs to formulate a policy which describes exactly what it wants to achieve. Each organisation needs its own policy which reflects its particular way of working: its activities and intentions, its size and budget, and the nature of its potential workforce, membership and constituency. But a policy is not going to change anything without a programme to put it into action. The first step is for the organisation to give someone, or a working group, the responsibility of formulating the policy and programme. It is an on-going responsibility which includes overseeing the implementation and monitoring of the programme.

If the policy is to succeed, it is essential that the management committee secures the informed support of all those affected by it. This particularly applies to the staff, whose job descriptions and contracts may have to change. If the staff are unionised, the formal support of the union shop is important. In practice this is unlikely to be a problem; in the voluntary sector it is often the unions which have taken the initiative in proposing EOPPs. All staff should be involved in discussing and commenting on draft proposals, whether in union meetings or staff meetings. The views of any consultative or policy-making body or forum should also be sought, so as to ensure maximum backing for the policy.

It is also worth discussing proposals with similar organisations which are already implementing EOPPs, and with local agencies representing people who will be affected by the policy, such as women and people with disabilities. If in doubt, ask a solicitor to check that the policy does not infringe the law.

The process of formulating a policy is essential to its

15

success. To offer a blueprint here, even if it were possible, would only encourage organisations to omit this process. What does follow is a guide to the issues which should be covered by a policy and programme.

 Your policy statement could be structured like this:

Statement of intent

This could include:
● Recognition that discrimination exists.
● The organisation's intention to eliminate discrimination in its policies and practices.
● The groups of people to whom the policy applies.
● A summary of what the organisation intends to do to implement the policy.

Procedures relating to recruitment, training and promotion

To include action the organisation intends to take to ensure that it complies with the law, offers genuine equality of opportunity and compensates for past discrimination.

Conditions of service

How these will take account of equal opportunities (for example, by offering improvements in maternity pay and leave).

Grievance and disciplinary procedures

There should be a clear procedure for dealing with a complaint from anyone who thinks that your organisation, or someone within it, is discriminating against them.

Training for equal opportunities

Special training will be required if the policy is to be implemented sucessfully. The policy should state the extent to which it should be available.

Examining existing procedures, monitoring and evaluation

What is being done to evaluate current practice, and the

position of groups of people who experience discrimination, within the organisation. The statement should make it clear how the programme is going to be monitored, who is responsible, how the results will be assessed and what action will follow.

*Policies relating to the management committee,
volunteers, members and users*

Measures to be taken to ensure that awareness of discrimination is translated into positive action within the wider context of the organisation's work.

Publicity

How the organisation's policy is to be made known to its members, users, potential job applicants and the public at large.

The rest of this chapter deals with the sometimes complex issues which have to be recognised, understood and dealt with when producing an EOPP.

Positive action

Positive action refers to the steps taken to counter the effects of past discrimination. For example, when women are under-represented in the workforce, positive active could include indicating in job advertisements, that women are particularly welcome to apply. It could also include advertising in publications aimed at women readers.

Positive action is not the same as positive discrimination, which would involve, in the instance given above, choosing a woman applicant in preference to a man, regardless of who was most suitable for the job. It is generally unlawful to discriminate in this way on grounds of sex or race. This is because legislation to protect the rights of women and Black people also makes it unlawful to discriminate against men and white people.

It is lawful to positively discriminate in favour of people who are registered as disabled. In fact, in some circumstances employers are required to discriminate in their favour.

Further information about the law is given in the relevant chapters.

Recruitment practice

Recruitment procedures should be scrupulously fair to ensure that applicants are considered strictly on merit. This requires a greater degree of formality than has usually been the practice in voluntary organisations. Informal recruitment methods give an unfair advantage to people who are already familiar with the organisation, feel comfortable with the people interviewing them and can make conversation by drawing on shared experiences. The result is discrimination against people from groups which are under-represented in the organisation.

A clear job description should be sent out with the application form. There should also be a personnel specification for the job, which is used in short-listing for interview and deciding who is offered the job. The personnel specification describes the qualities required from the person selected to do the job. It is usual to divide them into essential and desirable. One quality which should always be included is the ability to adhere to the organisation's EOPP. More information on job descriptions and personnel specifications is included in *Equal Opportunity Employment Policies: Guidelines for Voluntary Organisations*. (See Recommended Reading at the back of this book.)

Preliminary, informal interviews should only be held if they are considered to be strictly necessary. If this is so, careful thought should be given as to what they are intended to achieve, how they are conducted and how they fit into the decision-making process. This should be explained to the candidates in advance.

The short-listing panel and interviewing panel should be as diverse as possible in their membership. Your organisation may want to stipulate that they should always include at least one woman and one Black person. If there is no-one suitable within the organisation, someone from outside could be brought in.

Those conducting the interviews should be briefed on what questions should be avoided on the basis that they may indicate an intention to discriminate. A list of questions to be put to all candidates should be drawn up, and agreement reached on who will ask which questions and how they will be followed up with further questioning. Someone with responsibility for monitoring the EOPP should sit in on the interviews to check that the agreed procedures are properly followed.

Immediately after the interviews, notes should be made on how each candidate measured up to the personnel specification. This will make it possible to explain to unsuccessful candidates where they did well and badly, which may help them when applying for other jobs. It will also enable the organisation to respond to any challenge which may be made that it has discriminated unlawfully.

Finally, there should be clear agreement among members of the panel on how the final decision is to be made, if there is not consensus. Whatever method is used, it should take account of the situation which could arise if, for example, the only woman on the panel objects to the most favoured candidate on the grounds of his sexism.

Grievance and disciplinary procedures

A grievance procedure is a procedure by which someone can make a complaint against your organisation and have it investigated. The person making the complaint could be someone who uses your services, an unsuccessful job applicant or even a member of staff. The complaint could be against the organisation or a particular person.

A disciplinary procedure is a procedure for the employer to take action when someone's work or conduct has been found to be unsatisfactory.

All organisations employing staff should establish grievance and disciplinary procedures to deal with a variety of situations which may occur, only some of which will have equal opportunities implications. Advice on disciplinary procedures is given in *Discipline at Work: An ACAS Advisory Handbook*. (See Recommended Reading at the back of this book.)

Training

Special training is necessary for staff, and others, involved in implementing the EOPP. People should have the opportunity to learn about why the EOPP is needed and what it is intended to achieve. It is also important that they have the chance to air their doubts and anxieties and to think them through in a situation where they will not be silenced by disapproval, or ruled out of order. But training has limitations: oppressive attitudes cannot be eliminated overnight and training by itself does not change anything.

Training should aim to explain the general philosophy of equal opportunities and the meaning of specific terms such as discrimination, positive action, job-sharing, racism, sexism etc. For every oppressed group given consideration, training could cover the following areas:

1 General information about the group (e.g. for people with disabilities this could include the nature of disabilities, numbers of people affected etc).

2 The situation of that group in society – how they are discriminated against.

3 Course participants' experience of the oppression – whether as members of the group or 'from the other end' (e.g. white people looking at how they were taught racist attitudes).

4 Consideration of what action needs to be taken to change things. Methods used can include video, lectures, group exercises, role play and discussion.

Training can be expensive, but does not have to be. The lowest cost option is to do it yourself: someone from the organisation can explain the policy and facilitate discussion groups; speakers can be invited from local organisations, and their words can be backed up with free leaflets obtained from the Commission for Racial Equality, Equal Opportunities Commission and the Department of Employment. (See Useful Organisations at the back of this book.)

However, there are advantages to using professional trainers. They are familiar with the difficulties which can arise and experienced in handling them. They can also be more ambitious in the methods they use, making the course more interesting and effective. Small organisations can combine forces with others, or perhaps persuade an 'umbrella' group, such as the local Council for Voluntary Service, to put on courses.

It is also possible to arrange for consultants to devise a course especially to meet the needs of your organisation. This has the advantage of the participants actually talking to, and thinking with, the people they work with. They will then be more likely to put ideas, generated during the training session, into action.

People involved in recruitment and management of staff will require additional training in understanding legislation, such as the Sex Discrimination Act and the Race Relations Act, and on such issues as eliminating bias from interviews and job evaluation. People who have been on the receiving end of discriminative practices, can receive special training to help them gain the confidence and skill to equip them for more senior posts.

What is available

Training in equal opportunities is relatively new and is still being developed. Racism awareness training is fairly established, as is positive action training for women, such as assertiveness training and training in management skills. Courses in sexism awareness and disability awareness are less easy to find, as is training which deals with heterosexism and homophobia (see Chapter Six). Classism awareness training appears to have not yet got off the ground. But don't be put off; someone has to make a start and it is interesting to be innovative.

The best way to find suitable trainers, is to ask other voluntary organisations and employers with EOPPs about the people they have used. Non-evaluative (and incomplete) lists of trainers appear in *Implementing Equal Opportunities Policies* and *Directory of Race Relations and Equal Opportunities Trainers*. (See Recommended Reading at the back of this book.)

Controversy and criticism

Training in equal opportunities invariably stirs up strong feelings in participants and commentators. Examing one's own attitudes can be painful and confusing, and it is difficult for people who have been oppressed, to listen to others deny that they have oppressive attitudes. If people from the oppressed group are in a minority, or employed in low status jobs, they may feel unable to speak up. Careful consideration should be given to finding the most constructive way to handle these issues. Using racism awareness training as an example, should the training course be led by a Black person or a white person? A Black person and white person working together may be best able to offer leadership and safety to both groups. But there are no hard and fast rules. Much depends on the awareness, experience and approach of the trainer(s). Certainly, if the course is mixed, then for some of the time people should work with their own groups. This will allow Black people to share their discomfort at listening to yet more white racism, and white people to raise issues they might not feel able to in a mixed group.

Two or three consecutive days are needed for thorough training in racism awareness. Preferably there should be a follow up session a few weeks later to determine whether the initial session has led to effective action.

Criticisms have been made of a specific method of training known as Racism Awareness Training (RAT). These criticisms also have implications for different methods, and for training in other areas of equal opportunities. Among them is the charge that it deals with racism as though it exists in a world of its own, rather than considering it in the context of other oppressions, with which it is closely linked, such as classism. Another criticism is that by admitting to racism in these sessions white people are able to 'purge themselves of their guilt', without necessarily doing anything to change the situation.

It is worth talking to other organisations about their experience of training, to different consultants and having discussions among the staff, before embarking on an expensive and time-consuming training programme. It is undoubtedly true that awareness training will be of little, if any, use to the organisation unless it is linked to the implementation of an EOPP. It is also true that the EOPP is going to run into difficulties if training is ignored. The two are dependant upon each other to work effectively.

Examining existing procedures, monitoring and evaluation

Before it can decide what needs to be changed, the organisation has to examine its existing procedures. To take recruitment of staff as an example; where are jobs advertised, are job-sharers invited to apply and how is the interview panel chosen? Answers to these questions will indicate what changes should be considered. Data of a statistical nature is also needed. Does the proportion of people on the staff with disabilities correspond with their proportion in the population of working age? Are women adequately represented at management level? It is worthwhile looking at application forms from the previous year, to see who is applying for jobs with the organisation. Data can also be collected on other aspects of the agency's work, such as the composition of the management committee, of clients and members or those using its services.

Having established a base line, progress in implementing the policy can then be monitored by continuing to collect statistical data and comparing it with past results, on an annual basis.

Monitoring exercises raise a number of issues, both practical and ethical, which need to be dealt with. Collection of information about the position of women in the organisation will present no problem. Similarly it will be relatively easy and uncontroversial to gather statistics on the age range of employees, applicants, clients etc., should the organisation decide to do so. Accurate information about people with disabilities is hard to come by, as many disabled people do not register. The Department of Employment (DOE) recommends doubling the number of people registered to get a truer figure.

It is possible to collect data on ethnic background, with the co-operation of those concerned. This has been a controversial issue, but it is now generally accepted by organisations representing people from ethnic communities that, provided it is linked to a genuine intention to eradicate discrimination, it can be justified and is worthwhile. This does not mean, however, that organisations wishing to carry out ethnic monitoring will not find that employees are strongly opposed to it. To reach a satisfactory solution the issue should be raised and dealt with, well in advance of the date the monitoring exercise is intended to begin.

If agreement is reached, information can be gathered from existing employees, management committees etc., by circulating a questionnaire.

In order to gather information about job applicants, it is necessary to ask them to fill in a form, defining their ethnic background. This should be on a separate piece of paper from the application form. It should be accompanied by an explanation of why the information is needed, and how it is going to be used, and a statement of the organisation's Equal Opportunities policy. Only one person in the organisation should see the returned application and monitoring forms together. They should be separated before the application forms are circulated to those who need to see them, and the ethnic backgrounds of the applicants kept confidential.

A classification system is necessary. The CRE recommends this as a basic system:

Black	Afro-Caribbean origin African origin Asian origin Other – please specify
White	European origin including UK Other – please specify

This is preferable to a system which puts the emphasis on place of birth (which does not necessarily correspond with colour) or nationality (which has implications of 'belonging' or 'not belonging').

A more detailed classification could include the following groups:

African	Afro-Caribbean or West Indian/Guyanese
Arab	Bangladeshi
Chinese	Indian
Irish	Jewish
Pakistani	White
Mixed origin – please specify	Other – please specify

Another possibility is to simply ask the question, 'How would you define yourself by ethnic origin?' and let people choose their own categories.

The monitoring form should also be used to collect other relevant data, such as the numbers of people with a disability. People with a previously undisclosed history of 'mental illness', will have to be very sure of the good intentions of the organisation, and the confidentiality of the process, before disclosing this information. This is especially true if they are seeking employment, and is a consideration that also applies to lesbians and gay men.

Some organisations are attempting to analyse the people they are in contact with, according to their class background. Probably the best method is to ask:

Do you consider yourself to be:

working class	middle class
upper class	none of the above

This can be accompanied by an acknowledgement that people may choose to define their class position on the basis of family background, current economic status (eg. unemployed, unpaid houseworker, 'white collar' worker), or cultural identity. People who do not feel sufficiently part of the mainstream culture to belong to a social or economic class, should have the opportunity of answering 'none of the above'. A similar procedure can be used to collect information about the organisation's members.

All the information collected can be studied at an annual review by a working group, possibly of some staff and members of the management committee, or union representatives and management. It should give a good indication of how successful the programme is proving and in which ways. This is turn will indicate what steps need to be taken over the next year, in order to make further progress.

Budgeting

EOPPs cost money. It is worth recognising this fact, so that expenditure can be anticipated and an effort made to raise the money required. Grant applications should include an element for equal opportunities work. Training can be expensive and advertising jobs more widely, will cost the organisation more. A decision to extend the organisation's services to include currently under-represented groups will also involve additional costs. The organisation needs to decide how much it can afford to spend each year, and its priorities. This can be done at the same time as the annual review of the progress of the EOPP.

Publicity

Generally, the more it is known that an organisation has an Equal Opportunities policy, the more likely it is that people from previously under-represented groups will want to work for it, or otherwise become involved in its activities. It is also more likely to attract people who are interested in seeing such policies succeed. It is usual practice to draw attention to the policy in job advertisements by means of a short statement.

Here are some examples:

● Dudley Law Centre is an equal opportunities employer.

● The British Union for the Abolition of Vivisection is committed to becoming an equal opportunities employer. We welcome all applications regardless of race, nationality, sex, marital status, sexuality, disability or age.

● The New Cross Playbus Association aims to work towards positive equality of opportunity in relation to race, gender, sexual orientation, and disability.

● AXLE Co-operative Housing Services is committed to an Equal Opportunities Policy and especially welcomes applications from people who are likely to suffer discrimination.

Women

Opportunities for women to work outside the home have increased significantly in recent years. One factor has been greater knowledge about birth control, combined with improved methods, resulting in smaller families. 45 per cent of the employed workforce are women. (*Employment Gazette*. September 1986.) But workplaces are still male dominated. The 1981 census showed that 98 per cent of secretaries, but only 21 per cent of managers, were female. Women's pay rates are, on average, less than three quarters of those of men. (*New Earnings Survey*, Part A. 1986.) Women tend to be restricted to certain types of work, which are under-valued compared with 'men's' work. 69 per cent of women workers do clerical work, cleaning or catering, or work in education or the health service. (*Women and Employment, A Lifetime Perspective*. Department of Employment. 1981)

Because they are still expected to do most of the child-care and housework, many women work part-time. 82 per cent of part-time workers are women. (1981 census.) Part-time jobs tend to be in the lowest grades. Those working less than 16 hours lose out on some basic rights; this affects about 16 per cent of women workers. *Women and Employment, A Lifetime Perspective*, as above.)

Women who have children may lose continuity in their employment, which could affect their chances of promotion rather more than it needs to. The skills they acquire in running a home are rarely, if ever, taken into account by employers. Women can find it hard to realise their full potential as workers. In general, as they are growing up, they are not encouraged to see paid work as being important to them in the way young men are, and tend to have lower expectations of themselves. They may have the ability, but lack confidence, after a lifetime of being made to feel that men know best. The attitudes of senior staff may discourage them from stepping outside work situations where women are in the majority. Sexual harassment has been identified as a further reason for women to feel a lack of confidence in the workplace.

In the voluntary sector women are well-represented in the workforce but under-represented in senior positions. One large national charity has found that 65 per cent of its staff are female, but only 18 per cent of those in the top grades. A survey entitled *The Position of Women Within Councils for Voluntary Service*, which divided jobs into six grades, found that women constituted 74 per cent of those employed in the bottom three grades, but only 29 per cent of those in the top three grades. (See Recommended Reading at the back of this book.)

Organisations intending to develop EOPPs for women, need to be familiar with the provisions of several Acts of Parliament which affect women's employment. They are:

THE LEGAL FRAMEWORK

● Sex Discrimination Acts 1975 and 1986.

● The Equal Pay Act 1970 as amended by the Equal Pay (Amendment) Regulations 1983.

● The Employment Protection (Consolidation) Act 1978, as amended by the Employment Act 1980 and the Employment Act 1982.

● The Social Security Act 1986.

The Sex Discrimination Act 1975

This Act makes discrimination against women or men on the grounds of sex, unlawful in a variety of situations, in particular, employment. It also makes discrimination against married people in employment practice unlawful.

The Act defines two sorts of discrimination: direct and indirect. Direct discrimination against a woman occurs when an employer treats her less favourably than a man because she is a woman. Indirect discrimination occurs when an employer applies a condition to a woman which applies, or would apply, equally to a man, but:

1 Is such that the proportion of women who can comply with it is considerably smaller than the proportion of men who can comply with it.

2 It is to the detriment of the woman in question because she cannot comply with it.

3 It cannot be shown by the employer to be justifiable, irrespective of the sex of the person to whom it is applied.

An employer was found to be indirectly discriminating against women by imposing an upper age limit of 28 on applicants for jobs of a certain grade. It was found that a considerably smaller proportion of women than men could comply with this condition, as many women in their twenties are out of the labour market raising families. The condition was not found to be sufficiently justifiable on other grounds.

Recruitment practice

In recruitment practice, employers cannot usually discriminate on the grounds of sex; in arrangements made for deciding who should be offered a job, in the terms offered, or by refusing to offer employment. For example, in most situations it is unlawful in job interviews to ask women but not men, about their domestic situations.

Employers can however, discriminate in recruitment when a person's sex is a 'Genuine Occupational Qualification' (GOQ) for the job. The employer can discriminate in choosing who is appointed but not in the terms offered. Situations where GOQ may apply are listed in the Act. Those most applicable to voluntary organisations are:

1 Some jobs in single-sex establishments (e.g. men's hostels). The onus is on the employer to show that the character of the establishment requires that the job in question be held by a person of the same sex as the residents. (Section 7 [2] [d].)

2 Where the holder of the job provides individuals with personal services promoting their welfare or education, or similar personal services, and those services can most effectively be provided by a woman (or a man). (Section 7 [2] [e].) A job which could come into ths category is counsellor for a rape crisis centre. The job does not have to consist entirely of work which fulfills the GOQ criteria.

According to the Act, a GOQ exception cannot be applied if there are existing female employees who are capable of carrying out the duties to which the exception would apply; whom it is reasonable to employ on these duties, and whose numbers are sufficient to meet the employer's likely requirements, without undue inconvenience.

Generally, therefore, it is easier for a small employer to make a case for a GOQ exception than one employing large numbers of people, as there is less scope for using existing staff to carry out the duties. Employers thinking of taking advantage of GOQ exceptions are advised to check wth their local Law Centre or the Equal Opportunities Commission (EOC). (See Useful Organisations at the back of this book.)

Positive action

The Act does not explicitly recognise the unequal status of women and men in society. Although it does, to some extent, protect women from discrimination, it also limits the action which can be taken to improve the position of women as this may be seen as discriminating against men. It is, for example, unlawful to set 'quotas' for the number of female employees in certain jobs, as that implies choosing women in preference to men who are better applicants – positive discrimination. It is lawful, however, to set 'targets'. This involves deciding how many women it would be desirable to have in certain jobs and taking the steps outlined below to find suitable women to apply for them – in other words, taking positive action.

Where particular work in the organisation has been done exclusively or predominately by men, within the previous 12 months, the employer can:

1 Provide access to facilities for training for that work to female employees only. (Section 48 [1] [a].)

2 Take steps to encourage women to take advantage of opportunities for doing that work. (Section 48 [1] [b].)

In practice, a small organisation, which does not have numbers of people doing the same job, can apply this provision if women are under-represented in the entire workforce.

The employer cannot, however, discriminate at the point of selection. In other words, women can be encouraged to apply for jobs predominantly done by men, but if a man also applies, and is the best candidate, he must be given the job.

Advertising

It is unlawful to place an advertisement which suggests an intention to discriminate, unless there is a GOQ exception. Then it is usual to quote the relevent section of the Act in advertisements; for example, 'Female nurse required for Well-Woman Project. Section 7 [2] [e] Sex Discrimination Act 1975 applies'.

Otherwise it is unlawful to suggest an intention to discriminate by, for example, advertising for 'An Office Girl' or 'A Doorman'.

But it is lawful for an organisation to take steps to encourage women to apply for a job (see [2] in the Positive Action section above). It can indicate in advertisements that applications from women are particularly welcome. An example of the wording which could be used is, 'Women are under-represented in senior management positions in the organisation and are especially encouraged to apply for this job. Section 48 [1] [b] of the Sex Descrimination Act applies.'

The EOC produces pamphlets which give more information about advertising and the law. (See Recommended Reading at this back of this book).

Treatment of present employees

It is usually unlawful for an employer to discriminate in affording access to opportunities for promotion, transfer, training or other benefits. It is similarly unlawful to discriminate in cases of dismissal or other unfavourable treatment.

But as mentioned in the Positive Action section, in some situations women-only training schemes are lawful. An employer can also offer special treatment to women in connection with pregnancy and childbirth (e.g. by providing maternity leave).

It is still lawful to discriminate in matters to do with pension schemes. Pensions can be granted to women and men at different ages. This is expected to change eventually, to bring UK law in line with EEC Directives on equal treatment in occupational pensions and social security schemes.

Sex Discrimination Act 1986

This Act strengthens and widens the scope of the 1975 Act. These are the changes most likely to affect voluntary organisations.

Small employers

Previously, organisations employing five or less people were excluded from the provisions of the Sex Discrimination Act. This no longer applies.

Retirement Age

It is no longer lawful for an employer to make a woman retire at an earlier age than her male colleagues. This means, in effect, that employers should set the same retirement age for women and men.

But they still qualify to receive the state pension at different ages, and can qualify to receive pensions from occupational pension schemes at different ages.

The Equal Pay Act 1970, as amended by the Equal Pay (Amendment) Regulations 1983

This Act makes it unlawful to discriminate between women and men, in pay and other terms in their contracts of employment. It requires women and men to be paid the same for:

1 Work of broadly the same nature.

2 Work given equal value under a job evaluation study.

3 Work of equal value in terms of the demands made.

The last requirement has only been in effect since 1st January 1984, when the Act was amended by the Equal Pay (Amendment) Regulations 1983. It is the most significant because it takes account of the all too common situation, where women are segregated from men, into low paid jobs. With this amendment it is possible for women to have their wages increased to the same level as those of men doing different jobs, but ones which make equal demands on the employee.

The Employment Protection (Consolidation) Act 1978, as amended by the Employment Act 1980 and the Employment Act 1982

Two aspects of this wide-ranging Act are relevant here: those affecting part-time workers and maternity rights.

Part-time workers

Legislation referred to earlier applies to all employees, regardless of the hours they work, as does the Race Relations Act. But this Act makes a distinction between those working 16 hours a week or more (full-time), those working 8-16 hours a week and those working less than eight hours a week (both part-time). Full-timers have more rights than those working 8-16 hours a week, and those working less than eight hours have very few rights indeed.

People working 8-16 hours a week can claim the following rights only after they have worked five years continuously for the same employer. The qualifying period for full-timers is in brackets. Those working less than eight hours a week are excluded:

● Able to claim unfair dismissal (two years).
● Able to claim statutory redundancy pay (two years).
● Able to claim maternity leave (two years).
● Right to time off for trade union activities (no qualifying period).

All employees qualify for the following, regardless of the hours they work or their length of service:

● Time off to carry out duties as trade union safety representatives.
● Protection from dismissal or victimisation for trade union membership of activities.

Maternity rights

Time off for antenatal care

All employees, including those working less than eight

hours a week, are entitled to paid time off for antenatal care, however recently they have started their jobs.

Right to maternity leave

Some women, working eight or more hours a week, have the right to take leave and return to their own job, or a similar job, after their babies are born.

To qualify, full-timers must have worked for the employer continuously for at least two years. Those working 8-16 hours must have worked for five years. Whether full-time or part-time, they must also be employed until the end of the 12th week before their baby is due. They have to inform their employer, in writing, at least 21 days before the absence begins, that they will be absent because of pregnancy and intend to return, and enclose a copy of the certificate of expected confinement. (Form MAT B1 obtained from the midwife or GP.)

They are then entitled to up to 40 weeks maternity leave, begining eleven weeks before the week of the birth and finishing 29 weeks after the week of the birth.

An employee who takes maternity leave usually has the right to return to the same job. But there may be circumstances where the employer can legitimately claim that it is not reasonably practicable to offer the old job back and offers suitable alternative employment. A woman who finds herself in this situation may have to accept the alternative employment, but as a first step should seek legal advice if she thinks she has been treated unfairly.

Organisations employing five or fewer people are under less of an obligation to take the employee back if it is not reasonably practicable to do so.

Right to complain of unfair dismissal

A woman cannot usually be dismissed because she is pregnant or for a reason connected with her pregnancy. If she has not been employed long enough to be protected against unfair dismissal under the Employment Protection (Consolidation) Act 1978 she may be protected by the Sex Discrimination Act 1975.

She can be dismissed if her condition makes it impossible for her to do her job adequately or it would be against the law for her to do that job while pregnant (e.g. working with radioactive material). But the employer must offer suitable alternative employment if it is available.

The Social Security Act 1986

This Act includes provision for the payment of Statutory

Maternity Pay (SMP). It is paid by the employer, who deducts it from the National Insurance (NI) contributions paid to the Collector of Taxes. There are two rates of SMP.

An employee is entitled to the lower rate of SMP (£34.25 a week for 1988/9) if she fulfills the following conditions:

1 She has worked for the employer for at least 26 weeks, without a break, up to and into the 15th week before her baby is due.

2 Her normal weekly earnings for the eight weeks up to the end of the 15th week before her baby is due must be no lower that the Lower Earnings Limit for paying NI contributions. (£41 a week for 1988/9)

3 She gives 21 days notice to her employer that she intends to stop work.

4 She produces medical evidence of the expected week of confinement (Form MAT B1).

5 She stops work.

She does not have to intend to return to work.

A qualifying employee normally recieves SMP for 18 weeks, and can choose, within limits, when she wants the Maternity Pay Period (MPP) to run. The first week may be not earlier than the 11th week before the Expected Week of Confinement (EWC), and not later than the sixth week before the EWC. The MPP must end not later than the end of the 11th week immediately following the EWC.

A woman qualifies for a higher rate of SMP if she works full-time and has worked continuously for the same employer for two years up to and into the 15th week before her baby is due. If she works 8-16 hours a week the qualifying period is five years. The higher rate is 90 per cent of her normal weekly earnings. It is subject to tax and NI as if it were pay. The higher rate is paid for the first six weeks of the MPP only. The lower rate is paid for the other 12 weeks.

A woman who does not qualify for the higher rate will receive the lower rate for the whole 18 week period.

A woman who does not qualify for SMP may be able to claim Maternity Allowance from the DHSS.

NB. The above section is a summary of some aspects of complex legislation which have a bearing on equal opportunities work. It should not be regarded as a definitive guide to the law. Further sources of information on the law are listed under Recommended Reading at the back of the book.

■ Action which can be taken to improve opportunities for women comes into five categories:

1 Removing all discriminative practices in recruitment,

promotion, training and job evaluation, and taking positive action, particularly to raise the number of women in senior posts.

2 Making sure the workplace is one where women can achieve their full potential as employees, by eliminating sexist behaviour.

3 Introducing flexible working arrangements and more part-time work so that women, (and men) can more easily combine employment with family responsibilities.

4 Improving on basic rights in situations particularly affecting women, e.g. part-time work and maternity leave.

5 Making additional provision for employees with family responsibilities.

Removing discrimination and taking positive action

Recruitment and promotion

Women may not have been encouraged to stay in the education system as long as men, or to be as committed to acquiring qualifications. Before insisting on particular educational qualifications for a job, employers should consider whether they are really necessary, bearing in mind that they may not reflect ability. They should also take into account the skills acquired in running a home. (It has been calculated by the Legal and General Assurance Society that in 1987 the commercial rate for a housewife's work was £19,253 pa.)

Age limits can indirectly discriminate against women as it may take a woman longer to acquire work experience than a man, because she has taken breaks for child-care.

During interviews women should not be asked questions which would not be asked of men, such as 'do you intend to have children?', or 'what arrangements do you have for childcare?' Interviewers should also guard against making unconscious assumptions about young women's marriage or childbearing intentions. All-male interviewing panels should be avoided.

There are likely to be more women applicants for jobs, if advertisements are placed in publications read mainly by women. If women are under-represented in a particular area of work the advertisement can be worded to say that women are particularly welcome to apply.

Training

Special training can be offered to women already working in the organisation to equip them to apply for more senior posts. This could include, for example, assertiveness training, or training in management skills.

Part-time workers should be offered the same training opportunities as full-timers. Training sessions should , wherever possible, be arranged at times suitable for people with family responsibilities. On residential courses, provision can be made for child-care.

Job evaluation

Bias should be avoided when grading jobs, whether carrying out a proper job evaluation exercise or taking a less formal approach. Women should be represented on working groups which evaluate jobs. Job segregation may mean that women are concentrated in jobs requiring different sorts of skills with different working conditions to those in jobs done predominately by men. Factors in the women's jobs should be assessed fairly in relation to those in the men's jobs. For example, a female typist will be required to show a high degree of concentration in her job. A male maintenance worker may have to use physical strength. For the job evaluation to be fair, a suitable weighting should be given to each of these factors.

Eliminating sexist behaviour

Sexist behaviour can include men treating women in a condescending way or making them feel unwelcome. It also includes sexual harassment. In a less direct way, it may involve how the organisation is structured, decisions are made and meetings run.

To deal with sexist behaviour it is necessary to make clear what is acceptable, how unacceptable behaviour should be reported and what the consequences will be. Men need training to understand what sexism is, why their behaviour might be offensive to women and how they can change. Women need the opportunity to discuss their experiences of sexism and learn how to deal with it effectively. In some voluntary organisations, women meet regularly to share their experiences, support each other and promote the interests of women within the organisation.

Sexual harassment of women by men in the workplace, is an issue which needs to be tackled. This does not refer to relationships which both people want, but to the imposition of unwelcome attention, particularly if it is by someone in a senior position. The authors of *Sexual Harassment at Work* define sexual harassment as involving, "repeated, unreciprocated and unwelcome comments, looks, jokes, suggestions or physical contact that might threaten a woman's job security or create a stressful or intimidating environment. Physical contact can range from touching to pinching through to rape".

The Equal Pay and Opportunities Campaign has produced guidelines for employers for dealing with sexual harassment. They are that, following discussions with trade unions where appropriate, employers should issue a written policy statement which makes clear the following:

1 Sexual harassment of an employee by any other employee will not be tolerated and is contrary to the employer's policy.

2 The employer will take prompt, corrective action upon becoming aware that incidents involving sexual harassment have taken place.

3 Sexual harassment will be grounds for disciplinary action.

4 Supervisors have an affirmative duty to maintain their workplace as being free of sexual harassment and intimidation.

5 Employees subjected to sexual harassment should report such conduct to a specified management figure.

6 Supervisors should immediately report any complaints of sexual harassment to a specified person.

7 The employer's policy and procedures to be followed will be communicated to employees as part of training and induction programmes.

Organisations with a collective structure will have to adapt these guidelines to suit their circumstances. It may be that someone on the management committee should be nominated to deal with complaints.

It is worth noting that sexual harassment may well constitute a criminal offence, as well as giving a right of civil action for trespass to the person. It may also be possible to lay a complaint against an employer to an industrial tribunal, under the Sex Discrimination Act 1975. Advice should be sought from a Law Centre or solicitor.

Flexible working arrangements and part-time work

What is being proposed here is a move away from the rigid, 'nine to five — five days a week' way of working, to arrangements which make it easier for people to combine their family responsibilities with employment. As these responsibilities still fall largely on women, this will improve their employment opportunities. As flexible working arrangements become more common, more men may be encouraged to take on child-care, housework and care for other family members. This in turn will make it easier for women to do paid work. Flexible working arrangements and the availability of part-time work can also improve job opportunities for people with disabilities, who might not be able to manage a regular working week. The following are ways in which flexible and part-time working can be adopted in an organisation.

Flexitime

Many small voluntary organisations already have an informal system of working flexible hours. When it is applied formally there is usually a 'core-time' in the day when everyone is expected to be at work. Otherwise people can work when they choose, usually within limits determined by when the building is open, provided they average a certain number of hours a week. Employees keep a record of their hours and are entitled to days off (usually with a maximum limit) if their hours build up.

Employees benefit in many ways from flexitime. It is easier for parents to take their children to school before setting off for work, and they can work shorter hours during school holidays or family emergencies. More generally, benefits include being able to avoid rush hours and simply being more in charge of one's own life. Employers benefit as well. Workers are more likely to stay late to finish a task. They are likely to feel more positive about the organisation, becoming more productive and staying longer in their jobs.

There are advantages to having at least a degree of formality to the system. If, for example, flexitime can be mentioned in job advertisements, women are more likely to apply. Similarly, if it can be explained to potential recruits in a way which makes them feel confident of their rights, women with family responsibilities are more likely to feel able to accept job offers. It also makes life easier for parents if they can leave early to attend a sick child, knowing they have the right to do so and that they need not feel guilty for letting the organisation down, or concerned that they are being criticised in their absence.

Creating part-time work

Many women cannot work full-time. Traditionally it has been the lowest paid, lowest status jobs which have been part-time but there is no reason why at least some higher paid, senior jobs should not be part-time. As well as creating new part-time jobs, employers could sympathetically consider requests from existing staff to work reduced hours. This could be arranged by creating two part-time jobs from a full-time one, or by creating a 'job-share'. (See below.) It may particularly suit women returning to work from their maternity leave.

Voluntary organisations generally get a good deal out of part-time workers. They often use their work time more effectively and spend relatively more time outside of working hours thinking about their jobs. However, it should be ensured that part-time workers are not exploited by being expected to work extra hours unpaid. In a situation of long-term, high unemployment it also makes sense for more jobs to be part-time. Part-timers however, should not be denied the same rights as full-time workers. This issue is dealt with in the next section.

Job-sharing

This is an effective way of increasing opportunities to work fewer hours than the traditional working week. It can be applied to jobs which are seen as needing to be full-time, and which are often the most interesting, demanding and highly paid.

In job-sharing two people share a job and the employer divides the salary and other benefits between them. The working week can be divided in a number of ways, such as working alternate days, or half the week each. Some overlapping time may be necessary. One example of job sharing in the voluntary sector involves the post of national development officer being shared by workers in different parts of the country. (*Job-sharing and Voluntary Organisations. NCVO. 1983.*) Job-sharing can be especially suitable for an organisation which has funding for one full-time worker only, as it can deal with the difficulty of the worker becoming isolated and ineffective. The essence of job-sharing is that responsibility for the job is shared. If duties are simply divided between the employees then job-splitting is a more appropriate term.

As with part-time work, employees in job-shares need to guard against finding themselves working too many extra, unpaid hours. Job-shares may be set up by two people applying for a job together; an employer pairing up two applicants; a person in a full-time post arranging to share with another, new worker; or two people already working for the organisation arranging to share one job.

The EOC identifies the advantages to employers as being:

1 There can be a reduction in staff turnover.

2 Increased efficiency as a result of the greater flexibility of staffing, e.g. the possibility of peak period coverage.

3 The availability of a wider range of skills than can be provided by one full-timer.

4 Job-sharing makes it possible to employ talented people who are not available for full-time work.

It sees the disadvantages as being:

1 A small addition to administration costs.

2 Increased need for communication time may be necessary in some jobs.

3 Increased supervision may be necessary.

4 Extra training costs.

Job-sharing increases job opportunities for women (and people with disabilities). Employers are, therefore, recommended to set up procedures for considering the suitability for job-sharing of all newly created and vacant posts. Advertisements for jobs which are found to be suitable, should invite potential sharers to apply. Existing postholders (including those returning from maternity leave) should be invited to propose that their jobs become shared.

Special arrangements for employees caring for dependants

For employees with family responsibilities there will always be occasions which cannot be planned for, when there is an extra workload. A combination of formal agreements and informal arrangements can best help workers to cope without having to give up their jobs.

Formal arrangements should include 'compassionate leave' or 'dependant care leave'. It can be granted in the event of a family crisis, or if a child or other dependant person is sick. It may contain elements of paid and unpaid leave.

Informal arrangements can include the employee doing some work at home, informal flexitime and part-timers or job-sharers changing their regular hours and days of work.

No written agreement can cover every eventuality, but it is important that it is made clear, by establishing guidelines, that workers are entitled to rearrange their work when the situation requires it.

A large voluntary organisation has found that its willingness to be flexible, when employees are coping with family problems, has raised staff morale and their level of commitment to the organisation. It has also encouraged men to take on a greater caring role.

Improving on basic rights

Part-timers

As the vast majority of part-time workers are women and as part-time workers have fewer rights than full-timers, women lose out. Employers should do all they can to treat part-timers as well as full-timers.

The best solution is to make as many part-time jobs as possible 16 hours a week or over, so that the postholders enjoy full-timers' statutory rights. It is then up to the employer to treat them equally in other ways. This may include providing equal access to training courses and occupational pension schemes, making benefits such as holidays and sick pay available on a pro-rata basis, and ensuring that redundancy agreements do not discriminate against part-timers.

For those working under 16 hours a week, employers should also improve on their statutory rights, where possible, to bring them into line with full-timers. All employees should be granted at least some time off for trade union duties and activities. It is desirable to stipulate only a two year qualifying period before part-timers are entitled to maternity leave, the higher rate of maternity pay and redundancy pay. But this involves extra cost to the employer, as the additional maternity pay cannot be deducted from NI contributions. Organisations employing less than 10 people can claim a rebate of 35 per cent of statutory redundancy payments. This rebate however, cannot be claimed for payments made to part-timers who had worked less than five years for the employer.

But part-timers should at least be offered maternity leave on the same basis as full-timers. Maternity pay and redundancy pay which are additional to the statutory minimum, and have been agreed for full-time workers, should be made available to part-timers on a pro-rata basis.

Maternity pay and leave and child responsibility leave

It is quite common for voluntary organisations (and other employers) to improve on the basic legal requirements for maternity rights, making it possible for more women to continue in employment after childbirth.

Some have introduced 'paternity leave' which allows the father to take additional leave shortly after the child is born. This arrangement does not, however, take account of situations where two women share responsibility as parents, or where a child is adopted by a heterosexual, gay or lesbian couple. Paternity leave can be replaced by 'child responsibility leave' which is available to someone who adopts a child or the partner of someone who bears or adopts a child.

Below are examples of the policies of two voluntary organisations:

A large national organisation

1 Employees are entitled to maternity pay after one year's continuous service.

2 Maternity pay will be payable as follows: six weeks on full pay and a further 12 weeks on half pay. The organisation expects that a pregnant member of staff who has no intention of returning after confinement will resign before taking advantage of this further twelve weeks on half pay.

3 At least one week before she proposes to return to work she must notify the organisation of her intention. The organisation may delay her return for up to four weeks on giving specified reasons, and she may delay it for the same period. (Note: the legal requirement is for the employee to give 21 days of notice of her return.)

4 Sympathetic consideration is given to requests for

reduced working hours (to a 5½ hour day), with no loss of pay, for the last four weeks before starting maternity leave, in earlier stages if there is a particular medical problem, and for the first four weeks after returning to work. Managers will do everything in their power to give pregnant women appropriate working conditions (e.g. no heavy lifting, or prolonged standing or sitting).

5 A member of staff will be allowed reasonable time off with full pay for attendance at ante-natal and post-natal clinics and this will not count against sick leave entitlement.

6 Wherever practicable, special efforts will be made to accommodate women who wish to return to work after maternity leave but wish to work part-time. If an employee thinks that she may wish to return to work in a part-time capacity, she should inform her Head of Department as soon as possible, preferably before the commencement of her leave period, but at least 12 weeks before her due date of return, in order that her request may be fully considered. Heads of Departments will, so far as is reasonably possible, try to arrange for the employee to return to her own post in a part-time capacity. Where this is not possible the Head of Department will, in consultation with the employee and personnel officer, investigate other possiblities of part-time employment which are consistent with the employee's experience and also with the organisation's needs. The Head of Department will reply to the request as soon as possible and in any case within 28 days. It should be emphasised that, although special efforts will be made, the organisation cannot guarantee that part-time work will be available. This section also applies to male members of staff who expect to become fathers.

7 Subject to a qualifying period of six months' service male members of staff will be granted two weeks paternity leave. This leave is not counted as part of the normal leave entitlement.

A Law Centre

1 The qualifying period for maternity leave is one year.

2 Where practicable, and with the agreement of the management committee, a worker will be entitled to return to work part-time.

3 Where a worker is returning full-time she will be entitled to 40 weeks' leave, with 26 weeks at full pay and 14 weeks at half pay.

4 Where a worker is returning part-time, she will be entitled to 40 weeks leave, with 20 weeks at full pay, six weeks at the prospective salary she will receive on returning to work, and 14 weeks at half the prospective pay.

5 Where maternity leave is taken, the worker will be

required to return to work for a period of not less that six months, failing which, all remuneration in excess of statutory entitlement must be repaid.

6 The worker must inform the mangement committee in writing, at least three weeks before the commencement of leave, if she intends to return to work.

7 Where a worker adopts a child or her or his partner bears or adopts a child, then provided the worker has been continuously employed for 52 weeks the following leave may be taken:

(a) Four weeks leave at full pay, to be taken at any time from the date of commencement of pregnancy up to three months after the birth or adoption.

(b) Where the worker's partner is returning to full-time work or to a course of full-time study, and the worker undertakes the sole or major responsibility for the day-time care of the child, they are entitled to 26 weeks leave with 16 weeks at full pay, and 10 weeks at half pay. This will commence within seven weeks of the date of birth or adoption.

8 Where leave is taken under [7] the worker will be required to return to work for a period of not less than six months, failing which, all remuneration must be repaid.

9 Where leave is taken under [7] (b) the worker must inform the management committee, in writing, at least three weeks beforehand, that her or his partner is returning to full time work, or a course of study, and that s/he proposes to take extended leave.

10 Where leave is taken under [7] (b) the worker must inform the management committee in writing at least three weeks before the commencement of leave that s/he intends to return to work.

Additional provision for employees with family responsibilities

In the absence of state provision, employers can be of great assistance to their workers by providing nurseries on the premises, or by paying additional 'dependant allowances'. A dependant allowance is a payment which is additional to the basic salary and is made for each person who is dependant on the wage earner's income. This could include children, adults with no other income, and elderly or infirm relatives. The payment of dependant allowances should be given particular consideration by organisations with pay parity (i.e. all workers receiving the same basic wage). This is especially important if the level of pay is low, as otherwise they may find it virtually impossible to attract people with family responsibilities to the staff and keep experienced workers who take on family responsibilities.

Another possibility is to pay child-care costs when employees are required to work outside of their usual hours.

The lack of child-care facilities is a significant barrier to equality of opportunity for women. One solution is workplace nurseries. If your organisation cannot afford to set one up on its own, or does not have sufficient staff with young children, it could consider combining forces with other employers in the area. Information and advice can be obtained from The Workplace Nurseries Campaign. (See Useful Organisations at the back of this book).

4

People from ethnic communities

This is an issue about which it is particularly easy for confusion to arise in the use of language and, as mentioned in the introduction, definitions are constantly evolving and changing. For example, 'ethnic minority', 'racism', and 'black' are not always used to mean the same thing. Two principles have been followed here. The first is to attempt to use the language most favoured by those to whom it refers. The second is to say what is meant by the different expressions used.

'Ethnic community' is used here to refer to groups which have a distinctive identity within the majority culture, and which experience discrimination. This identity may be based on any of the following:

1 Traditions and customs.

2 Religious beliefs.

3 Where they or their ancestors came from.

4 The reasons why they or their ancestors came to Britain.

5 Their relationship with the majority culture.

6 Skin colour.

Their identity can, then, be based both on positive factors to do with valuing differences and traditions, and negative ones, to do with lack of acceptance by others. 'Ethnic community' is prefered here to the term 'ethnic minority', as perhaps emphasising the more positive aspects of maintaining a distinctive culture.

There is no definitive list of ethnic communities. Opinions differ. Certainly it includes people of Afro-Caribbean origin, and from India, Pakistan and Bangladesh. It will also include Jews, Irish people, Travellers, people from the Mediterranean countries such as Greece and Turkey, and many more.

Skin colour is an important issue here. People from ethnic communities in Britain are often (but not always) dark skinned, and experience discrimination which is based on skin colour. This discrimination is rather misleadingly called racism. Misleading because the term implies the existence of distinctive, racial groups with measureable biological differences. While it is true that people from different parts of the world often look different from each other, particular biological characteristics have never been found to be exclusive to one group of people. We are not all the same, but there is only one race – the human race. What is needed is a new word to mean 'discrimination based on skin colour'. Meanwhile we will have to make do with the rather unsatisfactory 'racism'.

People who experience racism may define themselves as Black (with a capital B), even though they come from different continents, have different cultures, and, to some extent, experience racism in different ways. The use of the term 'Black' is a political expression of solidarity, and a recognition of the shared experience of being on the receiving end of racism in Britain. 'Black' includes people whose origins can be traced back to Africa (which includes people from the Caribbean and Afro-Americans) and Asia, and those from other parts of the world who may choose to define themselves in this way (such as people from China, Iran or Malaysia).

It is important to recognise that if it were not for the racism of white people, Black people would define themselves according to their countries of origin, cultural identity, or simply as members of the human race.

Elsewhere 'black' (with a small b) may be used in a narrower sense, to mean people whose origins can be traced back to Africa. It may also be used to include people from the Indian sub-continent. Sometimes 'black' and 'ethnic minority' are used to mean the same thing, which can be confusing.

This chapter is mainly about equal opportunities for Black people, but is also concerned with the rights of people from ethnic communities who are white.

Black people are disadvantaged compared with white people before they even begin to apply for jobs. Discrimination in education and training schemes (which is well documented) makes it harder to obtain qualifications. Housing policies, and the effects of past discrimination by employers, can leave Black people trapped in decaying inner city ghettos where the job market is dwindling.

Black people then face direct discrimination from potential employers. In 1986 the Manpower Services Commission (MSC) did a survey of people using job centres, for whom interviews were arranged. The results showed that 26 per cent of white, but only 12 per cent of people of Afro-Caribbean or Asian origin were offered a job. In a research project in Nottingham, identical letters were sent by equally well-qualified white and

Afro-Caribbean and Asian applicants, to over 100 firms advertising 'white-collar' jobs. Almost half interviewed the white candidate but refused to see an Afro-Caribbean or Asian person. (*Half a Chance? CRE. 1980.*)

The effect of this discrimination is that the proportion of Black people in low paid, unskilled jobs, working unsociable hours is higher than for white people, and unemployment is also higher.

Unemployment for Black workers is twice as high as for white workers. A study of men with 'O' levels found nine per cent of white men, 18 per cent of Asian men and 25 per cent of West Indian men to be unemployed. (*Labour Force Survey.* Department of Employment. 1985.) Research into the employment of graduates from the non-university sector of higher education, found that less than half of Black graduates were in full time employment 12 months after graduating, compared with 70 per cent of white graduates. (*Employment of Graduates from Ethnic Minorities.* CRE. 1987.)

The differences between white and Black women workers are less marked because of the discrimination experienced by all women. But a survey in the London Borough of Haringey revealed that, for the Black women interviewed, it was harder to find a job, even though they had more qualifications than the white women. White women were, therefore, doing similar work to Black women who had better qualifications. (*Survey of Unemployed Women in Haringey.* Haringey Women's Employment Project. 1984.) Results from the MSC survey of job centres, suggest that Black women face more discrimination on the grounds of race, than on the grounds of sex.

After overcoming the barriers to recruitment, Black people still have to contend with racism in the workplace. At its most blatant, it may be in the form of harassment and insults; or white people may refuse to co-operate with a Black worker. Even in the most well-meaning voluntary organisation, Black people may have problems with white workers. In some ways the subtle racism perpetuated by well-intentioned white people may be more difficult to deal with.

An organisation in which all the workers are white may decide that its priority in implementing an anti-racist policy is to employ a Black worker. The interviews are conducted in a way which is objective and fair. A Black worker is appointed on merit. The white workers and management committee are pleased with themselves for having visibly shown themselves to be anti-racist. But they do not really expect the Black worker to do the job as well as a white person. They interfere, take away responsibilities and generally undermine the person's confidence and ability to do the job (eventually proving themselves to be 'right'!).

There are other ways in which Black workers can become isolated in predominantly white organisations. They may be the people expected to do most of the work in implementing an anti-racist policy:

liaising with the local Council for Racial Equality, organising activities for Black clients and giving talks to Black people about the organisation's work. They can then end up working quite separately from the white workers and feel they have little in common.

Workers in voluntary organisations often spend time together outside of work hours discussing their jobs. Black people can feel excluded from these gatherings for many reasons, which could be as blatant as the white workers not realising that the pub they go to after work is not welcoming to Black people.

Ways can be found of dealing with these problems and differences can be turned into positive assets. What is required is a willingness to acknowledge and deal with problems, even if it feels painful and difficult to do so.

■ ## The Race Relations Act 1976

This Act is similar in form to the Sex Discrimination Act of 1975 and has much the same strengths and weaknesses. For convenience, some information which applies to both Acts is repeated here.

The Act makes discrimination on racial grounds unlawful in a variety of situations, in particular, employment. 'Racial grounds' is taken to mean on grounds of colour, race, nationality (including citizenship), or ethnic or national origins. Because the Act refers to 'racial groups' rather than ethnic communities, that expression is used, with reservations, in this section on the Act.

The Act defines two sorts of discrimination: direct and indirect. Direct discrimination occurs where an employer treats a person less favourably, on racial grounds, than s/he treats someone else. Indirect discrimination occurs when an employer applies a condition, to a person of one racial group, which applies, or would apply, equally to a person not of the same racial group as the other, but:

1 Is such that the proportion of persons of the victim's racial group who can comply with it, is considerably smaller than the proportion of persons not of that group who can comply with it.

2 It is to the detriment of the person in question because s/he cannot comply with it.

3 It cannot be shown by the employer to be justifiable, irrespective of the colour, race, nationality, or ethnic or national origins of the person to whom it is applied.

An employer in an area with a high proportion of Black residents could be found to be indirectly discriminating in recruitment, if the existing workforce was virtually all white and recruitment was by word of mouth. In practice this would mean that Black people did not have the same opportunity to apply for the available jobs as white people.

Recruitment practice

In recruitment, employers cannot usually discriminate, on the grounds of race; in arrangements made for deciding who should be offered a job, in the terms offered, or by refusing to offer employment. For example, if Black applicants were asked in interviews, 'Are you sensitive to racial jibes?' or, 'How do you feel about working for an all white organisation?', the employer would be discriminating in the arrangements made for deciding who is offered the job. The Black applicants would be put in a difficult situation, which would not apply to white people.

Employers can however discriminate in recruitment where being of a particular racial group is a 'Genuine Occupation Qualification' (GOQ) for the job. The employer can discriminate in choosing who is appointed but not in the terms offered. Situations where GOQ may apply are listed in the Act. The situation most applicable to voluntary and community organisations, is where the job holder provides people of the racial group in question with personal services promoting their welfare, and those services can most effectively be provided by a person of the same racial group. (Section 5[2] [d].) A situation where this could apply is a Victim Support Scheme employing a Black person to visit victims of racial harassment.

The job does not have to consist entirely of work which fulfills the GOQ criteria.

According to the Act, a GOQ exception cannot be applied if there are existing employees of the appropriate racial group, who are capable of carrying out the duties to which the exception would apply; whom it is reasonable to employ on these duties, and whose numbers are sufficient to meet the employer's likely requirements, without undue inconvenience.

Generally, therefore, it is easier for a small employer to make a case for a GOQ exception, than one employing large numbers of people, as there is less scope for using existing staff to carry out the duties. Employers thinking of taking advantage of GOQ exceptions are advised to check with their local Law Centre or Council for Racial Equality.

Positive action

The Act does not explicitly recognise the unequal status of different racial groups in society. Although it does, to some extent, offer protection to people from racial groups which experience discrimination, it also limits the action which can be taken to improve their position, as this may be seen as discriminating against other racial groups. It is, for example, unlawful to set 'quotas' for the number of people from a particular racial group in certain jobs, as that implies choosing people from that racial group in preference to others who are better applicants – positive discrimination. It is lawful, however, to set 'targets'. This involves deciding how many people from a particular racial group it would be desirable to have in certain jobs and taking the steps outlined below to find suitable people to apply for them – positive action.

If people from a particular racial group have been under-represented among those doing particular work in an establishment at any time in the last 12 months, the employer can:

1 Provided access to facilities for training for that work to people from that group only. (Section 38 [1] [a].)

2 Take steps to encourage people of that racial group to take advantage of opportunities for doing that work. (Section 38 [1] [b].)

'Under-represented' can mean in comparison with either the proportion of that group among all employees in the establishment, or with the population of the area from which the employer normally recruits for work at the establishment. The Act refers to establishments, because large employers can have different places of work in different localities. Each is treated separately, for the purposes of the Act.

In practice, a small organisation, which does not have numbers of people doing the same job, can apply this provision if people from a particular racial group are under-represented in the entire workforce, relative to the proportion of that racial group in the local population.

The employer cannot, however, discriminate at the point of selection. In other words, people from a particular racial group can be encouraged to apply for jobs if they are under-represented, but the job must go to the best candidate who applies.

In the Race Relations Act there is an additional provision for positive action which does not have an equivalent in the Sex Discrimination Act. It is not unlawful to provide persons of a particular racial group with special access to facilities or services to meet the needs of that group in regard to their education, training or welfare, or any ancillary benefits, provided they have a special need which is met by such provision. This extends the right to provide special training beyond [1] above.

Advertising

It is unlawful to place an advertisement which suggests an intention to discriminate, unless there is a GOQ exception. Then it is usual to quote the relevant section of the Act in advertisements; for example, 'Bangladeshi community worker required for project on predominantly Bangladeshi council estate. Section 5 [2] [d] of the Race Relations Act 1976 applies'.

Otherwise it is unlawful to suggest an intention to discriminate. This applies to advertisements which include requirements that indirectly discriminate. For example, requirements that applicants have language skills, or academic qualifications, or are of a particular religious faith, when it cannot be justified as necessary to do the job.

But it is lawful for an organisation to take steps to encourage people of a particular racial group to apply for a job (see [2] in the Positive Action section above). It can indicate in advertisements that applications from people of that racial group are especially welcome. An example of the wording a small organisation might use is 'People of Asian origin are currently under-represented in the workforce and are especially encouraged to apply for this job. Section 38 [1] [b] of the Race Relations Act 1976 applies'.

The Commission for Racial Equality (CRE) produces pamphlets which give more information about advertising and the law. (See Recommended Reading at the back of this book.)

Treatment of present employees

It is usually unlawful for an employer to discriminate in affording access to opportunities for promotion, transfer, training or other benefits. It is similarly unlawful to discriminate in cases of dismissal or other unfavourable treatment. But, as mentioned in the Positive Action section, there are some situations where training schemes for workers from a particular racial group are lawful.

ACTION
MPLOYERS ■ In addition to following the requirements of the law, organisations can take further action to offer genuine equality of opportunity to people from ethnic communities. This comes into three categories:

1 Removing all discriminative practices and taking positive action to recruit workers from ethnic communities, particularly to more senior positions.

2 Ensuring that contracts of employment take full account of the needs of people from ethnic communities.

3 Taking steps to make the workplace one where people from ethnic communities feel welcome, and are able to work to the best of their ability, unhindered by racist attitudes.

Removing discriminative practices and taking positive action

To see what steps need to be taken, it is first necessary to identify how your organisation is discriminating against people from ethnic communities.

One way this can occur is in the requirement of particular educational qualifications from applicants for a job. While this may sometimes be necessary, it does not take account of the position of people who may have 'under-achieved' at school because of moving from one country to another or because English is not their first language. It may also deter people who acquired their qualifications abroad.

Employers who advertise in journals which are predominantly read by white people should not be surprised if few Black people respond to them. They should also consider the effect of an all-white interview panel on a Black applicant. How confident would a white person feel if s/he was interviewed for a job with an organisation which only employed Black people, by an all-Black panel, and s/he was the only white candidate? If that situation is reversed, and the additional factor of white racism included, then the Black candidate can hardly be expected to perform at her or his best.

People generally apply for jobs with organisations they want to work for and when they think their application has some chance of success. People from ethnic communities are not likely to feel encouraged on either count, if your organisation has not demonstrated any awareness of racism in its policies.

These, then, are some steps which can be taken to deal with discrimination and to positively encourage people from ethnic communities to apply for jobs in your organisation:

1 Educational qualifications should not be required unless they are strictly necessary. 'Informal' experience, such as unpaid community work, personal experience of welfare services or knowledge of inner city problems should be valued. This should be made clear in advertisements and reflected in the application form. This will also benefit other groups which face discrimination, such as women and working class people.

2 Where educational qualifications are required it should be indicated in advertisements that equivalent qualifications obtained abroad will be fairly considered. Advice on such qualifications can be obtained from the National Equivalence Information Centre. (See Useful Organisations at the back of this book.)

3 All vacancies should be publicly advertised, otherwise they tend to go to people who are 'the same' (and that includes the same colour) as those already involved with the organisation. It is worth considering advertising in the ethnic community press. The CRE provides a free list. Details of vacancies can also be circulated to local organisations representing ethnic communities.

4 On job application forms, care should be taken to avoid any questions which may suggest an intention to discriminate. However unbiased you intend to be, potential candidates will make their own assumptions, based on past experiences of discrimination. Do you really need to know candidates' nationality and place of birth?

5 A brief statement of the organisation's Equal Opportunities policy should appear in advertisements, and a longer one should be enclosed with application forms and monitoring forms, with an explanation of the monitoring procedure.

6 It may be possible to take advantage of the positive action provisions of the Race Relations Act to especially encourage people from ethnic communities to apply for jobs. In some instances it will be possible to specify that the postholder is from a particular ethnic community, on the grounds that it is a GOQ for the job. If the GOQ exception does not apply, it may still be lawful to indicate that the postholder will be working with people from a particular ethnic community, and that experience and knowledge of that group is required. If fluency in a language such as Bengali or Mandarin would be an advantage, then that too can be indicated.

7 Your organisation is more likely to be able to advertise along these lines, if it has thought through the implications of the need to combat racism in its policies and working methods, and has taken action. If it is offering a service which is not being used by people from ethnic communities, it can initiate special projects to involve these groups. This is itself an important ingredient of an EOPP. It will also make your organisation more attractive to job applicants from ethnic communities.

Contracts of employment

People from different ethnic communities have special needs which should be taken into account in contracts of employment, if they are to receive equal treatment.

A number of public holidays coincide with Christian Festivals, such as Christmas and Easter. Workers who have other religious beliefs or traditions may prefer to work on those days and take time off for occasions which have meaning for them. For example, Jews might want to take Yom Kippur as a holiday and Sikhs will want to commemorate the birthday of Guru Nanak. A benefit of some people working on public holidays is that they can keep a service going which would otherwise have to close down for the day. If it is not practicable to keep the building open it may be possible to make arrangements for people to work at home. The CRE distributes a free calendar of religious festivals. (See Useful Organisations at the back of this book.)

Muslims need to be able to pray at certain times of the day. Over Ramadan (which lasts one lunar month) Muslims fast during daylight hours and may find it difficult to work a full day during that period. Flexible working hours can help Muslims with both these practices. (See Chapter Three p.35.)

People from ethnic communities may want to visit relatives in their countries of origin from time to time. This is made easier if it is possible to accumulate leave over a period of more than a year, and to take additional, unpaid leave.

Eliminating racist behaviour

Blatant oppressive behaviour in the workplace can be discouraged by making it clear that racist insults, 'jokes' etc. are not acceptable. There needs to be a clear grievance procedure for anyone who has a complaint and a disciplinary procedure for dealing with the culprit.

More subtle and indirect racism is, in some ways, more difficult to eliminate. White people have to learn that, although it is not their fault, they are racist, however well intentioned they are; but that they can learn to change their behaviour. Some form of racism awareness training is necessary for that. It should be compulsory for people involved in the recruitment or management of staff. Black people can also benefit from opportunities to discuss with each each other, how they are affected by racism and how they can be effective in dealing with it. They may also find it supportive to meet regularly together, or with Black people doing similar work in other organisations.

Oppressive behaviour directed at people from ethnic communities who may be white should, of course, be regarded as equally unacceptable. Anti-Irish or anti-Jewish 'jokes' should, for example, be no more tolerated than those directed against Black people.

5

People with disabilities

A disability is a total or partial loss of a functioning ability. It has a different meaning from handicap, which is the disadvantage arising from that disability. A handicap is often greater than it need be because of discrimination against people with disabilities. Discrimination may be blatant and direct, such as an employer refusing a job interview; or indirect, with people being excluded from activities because their needs have not been taken into account. An example would be a wheelchair user being unable to consider working for an organisaton because its premises are not wheelchair accessible.

Disability is generally taken to include physical disability, learning difficulties, and mental distress. Accurately estimating the proportion of the population of working age who have a disability is not easy, but it could be as high as 10 per cent.

People with physical disabilities

Most people will experience some sort of physical disability during their lifetimes, particularly as they get older. Some will be temporary, such as a broken limb, and others, such as short-sight, need not cause much of a handicap. It is when a disability is severe and more or less permanent that coping with it becomes more difficult.

Physical disabilities may be genetic in origin, or caused by accident or illness. They vary greatly in the effect they have on people and the solutions required to restrict the degree of handicap. For instance, blind or partially-sighted people can tackle a wide range of work provided they receive suitable training and appropriate aids are available. Sickle Cell

53

Anaemia – an inherited condition which affects mainly people of African and Caribbean origin – causes a wide variety of physical problems which come and go. Availability of part-time work and flexible working arrangements may enable a person with this condition to be employed by the organisation.

Individuals will respond to the same disability in different ways, depending on the time in their life they first experience it, and their own ability to deal with the situation.

People with learning difficulties

These people have a degree of impairment to their intellectual abilities as a result of brain damage. They tend to prefer being described as having learning difficulties rather than a mental handicap. About one per cent of the population is affected in this way. Some people are born with the problem, others acquire it as a result of an accident or illness, such as Meningitis. The degree of impairment varies enormously.

People with learning difficulties often find that other people have given up on them and have assumed their condition is more limiting than it need be. Lack of confidence may then become as much of a problem as the underlying disability. Consequently, they can often respond well to training opportunities and encouragement.

Because the degree of disability varies so widely, people with learning difficulties have very different abilities and needs. Some will be able to handle many work situations. Others may only be able to do a limited range of work. For people with the most severe disability, some form of sheltered employment may be necessary.

Sheltered employment usually consists of manufacturing work in a unit which is subsidised by public funds. The workers receive special supervision, and are not expected to be as productive as those in commercial firms.

People are sometimes confused by the difference between physical disability and a learning difficulty. They may wrongly assume that someone with a physical disability has a learning difficulty as well.

But there are some conditions where both may be present. Downs Syndrome is a condition with genetic origins which causes learning difficulties. People with Downs Syndrome have a distinct physical appearance, which is not itself a disability, but may trigger a prejudiced response in others. In addition, they may have heart and respiratory defects which are a disability.

Cerebral Palsy is a condition usually caused by loss of oxygen to the brain during birth. There is a greater or lesser degree of physical disability, which may be accompanied by learning difficulties, depending on which part of the brain is affected.

Mentally distressed people

'Mental distress' is a term used to describe various disabling emotional states. It is preferred to 'mental illness' by many of the people who have been prescribed mood-altering drugs, seen a therapist or been a patient in a mental hospital.

A mentally distressed person may experience a degree of anxiety or depression which makes it hard, or impossible, to cope with day to day life. Less often, there may be a major disturbance in the person's thoughts and feelings, resulting in dramatic changes in behaviour and the development of beliefs which seem bizarre to others.

It is generally thought that 'mental distress' is caused by people's experiences of life, particularly in early childhood. Some people believe that the person's genetic make-up can also be a factor in the development of some forms of mental distress, but this has not been proved. The most common form of treatment is with mood-altering drugs, such as tranquillisers and anti-depressants. Many people recover, and others are able to cope in ways which avoid their employers even knowing of their difficulties.

People's distressed emotional states are often natural, human responses – grief, anger, despair or shock – to intolerable circumstances. To give this distress a medical label is to deny and disguise the nature of the cause. Counselling, therapy and self-help are seen by many people who have been treated by doctors and psychiatrists, as preferable to drugs, whch may make things worse.

'Mental illness' is to some extent culturally defined. Often a doctor from one of the groups which is given the most authority in this society (e.g. white or male) is in the position of diagnosing a patient from a group which experiences oppression (e.g. Black or female). The doctor's prejudiced attitude may cause her or him to fail to understand what the patient is experiencing. It is thought, for example, that this is one reason why a relatively high proportion of the Black population is diagnosed as schizophrenic by white psychiatrists.

Mental distress may arise from the effects of the oppressive practices and attitudes which EOPPs are intended to deal with. Women are twice as likely as men to be taking tranquillisers. Many people would agree that sexist conditioning – women being taught to undervalue themselves, accept mistreatment and turn their frustration and anger inward – is a major cause of anxiety and depression. Much of the mental distress experienced by men can be attributed to their early conditioning to hide their vulnerability and compete with each other.

People who are victims of discrimination are more likely to become mentally distressed. This means that an organisation has to offer equal opportunities to people who have experienced mental distress if they are to avoid discriminating against women, people from ethnic communities and others who are covered by their EOPP.

■ There is a great deal of ignorance, fear and confusion about disability. People with disabilities experience this as discrimination, including discrimination in employment. The Spastics Society tested employers of secretaries in the private sector by sending out what were effectively identical applications from people with and without disabilities. The results showed that able-bodied appicants were 1.6 times more likely to receive a positive response than disabled applicants. (*An Equal Chance for Disabled People?* The Spastics Society. 1986.)

The level of unemployment is far higher among people with disabilities than the rest of the population, and tends to be longer term. A survey showed that 26 per cent of unemployed people with disabilities had been out of work for more than two years, compared with eight per cent of the able-bodied unemployed. (*Review of Assistance to Disabled People.* MSC. 1982.) People with disabilities are also likely to be lower paid. Yet their living expenses are often higher as they may have additional needs, for example, the need for special diets.

■ **Disabled Persons (Employment) Act 1944 and 1958**

This legislation was introduced when there was a great deal of concern for those disabled during the war. It established a voluntary register of disabled people and places an obligation on employers with 20 or more workers to employ a quota of their workforce from the register. The quota is three per cent. It is not an offence to be below the quota but an employer in that situation must not engage anyone other than a registered disabled person without first obtaining a permit to do so. These may be issued by the local job centre if there are not suitable disabled people available.

However, the Act has not been properly enforced, and an increasing proportion of firms are being issued with permits. The situation in 1986 was that only 27 per cent of employers subject to quota were fulfilling it, and 56 per cent of those who were not had been issued with permits. (Figures from Disabled Persons Service. MSC.)

Registered disabled people currently account for only about one per cent of the total workforce, but that does not reflect the true number of people with disabilities. Many do not bother to register because they are already in work or do not expect registration to help them.

■ There is a wide variety of services and resources (such as financial aid and loans of equipment) available to employers wanting to offer employment opportunities to people with disabilities.

Disablement resettlement service

This service was provided by the Manpower Services Commission (MSC) until 1988. It is now provided by the Department of Employment, which has taken over the employment services which were provided by MSC. It can be contacted through your local Department of Employment office. The MSC has become the Training Commission. Disablement Resettlement Officers (DROs) maintain the register, encourage local firms to employ disabled people, assess the abilities of people with disabilities and try and find jobs for them, and provide information to employers and disabled people about schemes that exist to help them. These include:

1 *Job Introduction Scheme.* If an employer has doubts about taking on a person with a disability, or retaining an employee who becomes disabled, the Department of Employment will make a contribution to the cost of employing the person for a trial period of six weeks. The Royal Society for Mentally Handicapped Children and Adults offers grants to employers taking on people with learning difficulties for a trial period. (See Useful Organisations at the back of this book.)

2 *Capital Grants Scheme.* Grants are available towards the cost of adapting premises and equipment in order to enable a specific disabled person to be employed or retained. However, the employer cannot apply for the grant until the worker is in post and may then have to wait several months for the money to come through.

3 *Special Aids.* Special tools or equipment needed by a disabled person to overcome a handicap and obtain employment are issued to her or him on free, permanent loan.

4 *Release for training.* Financial assistance can be made available to an employer while a disabled worker is receiving special training.

Other sources of help and information

Further assistance can be given by various voluntary organisations. For example, the Royal National Institute for the Blind offers financial assistance for part-time readers for blind or partially-sighted workers; the Royal National Institute for the Deaf can arrange for an interpreter or lip reader to be present when a person who is deaf or hard of hearing is interviewed for a job.

The *Code of Good Practice in the Employment of Disabled People* has comprehensive details of sources of financial and practical help and information. (See Recommended Reading at the back of this book.)

Employers should ensure that they do not discriminate directly or indirectly against people with disabilities. They should consider taking positive action to offer opportunities which are denied elsewhere.

Recruitment

Organisations not required by law to positively discriminate in favour of people with disabilities, can still do so if they wish. The only exception would be if the organisation did so in such a way that it left itself open to a charge that it was a pretext for discriminating on grounds of sex or race. It is possible to discriminate in favour of people with disabilities who are unregistered, as well as those who are.

Organisations which represent or offer services to disabled people may be particularly interested in ensuring that their staff have had experience of disability themselves. For example, an agency running a day centre for psychiatric patients could see it as advantageous to have it staffed by people who are ex-patients themselves, provided of course they are suitably experienced and qualified in other ways.

Advertisements should make it clear that people with disabilities are welcome to apply and will be given fair consideration. There are more likely to be applications from disabled people if the local DRO and voluntary organisations concerned with disability are informed of vacancies.

Jobs descriptions and requirements in advertisements should not be impossible for disabled people to fulfil, unless it is strictly necessary. For example, applicants should not be required to have a driving licence if driving is only occasionally useful and could be avoided; otherwise blind and partially-sighted people will be excluded from consideration. It is important to be sensitive in asking questions about health and disability on application forms and in interviews. A person may understandably be wary of disclosing a disability, in case it means that s/he will not be fairly considered for the job.

The Code of Good Practice in the Employment of Disabled People gives guidance on this issue. (See Recommended Reading at the back of this book.)

It should not be assumed that candidates are able-bodied. Invitations to interview should ask candidates if they need any special assistance.

All voluntary organisations should aim to have premises which are fully wheelchair accessible. However, if this is not immediately possible it should not be assumed that wheelchair users will not find ways of managing. People with disabilities are used to surviving in hostile environments. Advertisements should state the degree of accessiblity of the premises.

Induction, training and promotion

Some disabled workers will have special needs to be considered when they start a job, such as a place where they can take medicine privately, or having a parking space near the premises reserved for their use. Any special arrangements for the person to leave the building in case of fire should be sorted out and the first-aid officer alerted to particular needs.

Employers should ensure that disabled workers are not excluded from training courses because their needs have not been taken into account. As far as promotion is concerned the issues are much the same as those dealt with in the section on recruitment.

Employees who become disabled

It makes sense for all concerned to do everything possible to help people in this situation to continue with their jobs. How the worker is first affected will depend on the nature of the disability. Some instances will inolve a long absence from work followed by a slow return; in other cases a progressively deteriorating condition will give the worker and employer time to adjust. The Disablement Advisory Service can offer an expert assessment of what the worker will be able to achieve. If the employee can continue with the most important aspects of her or his work, then the job description could be changed to take this into account. In some instances the best solution is for the disabled worker to move to another job in the organisation.

Many employers improve on statutory sick pay, by extending full pay for an additional period with a furher period on half pay. If the worker is no longer receiving sick pay, her or his contract will continue unless s/he is dismissed. This means s/he will retain employment status for contractual purposes, such as eligibility for redundancy pay.

A return to work will be made easier by flexible arrangements, such as starting by working at home, or building up hours gradually. A successful return to work is a key process in the rehabilitation of someone with a newly acquired disability.

Flexible working arrangements

These are not only a way of helping a newly disabled worker to continue in employment but, in general, provide more employment opportunities for disabled people. Some disabilities require people to take more rest; others mean that they need frequent medical appointments and others may vary in the severity of their effect, making it difficult to work at some times and easier at others. It has been estimated that there are 100,000 people who have a disability which disqualifies them from full-time work, but would enable them to do part-time work or work flexible hours. Flexible working arrangements are described on pages 35 to 38.

Awareness training

For people with disabilities to do their jobs effectively, it is important that they are treated respectfully and completely accepted by their colleagues. Often it is simply fear and embarrassment, stemming from ignorance, which gets in the way. Training in disability awareness should be made available to all employees. Those involved in management and recruitment should be fully aware of the needs and skills of people with disabilities. Workers who are about to be joined by a person with a disability should have the opportunity to learn about their disability and the particular needs of people with it, in advance.

Contracting out work

Facilities exist to provide work for people with disabilities who are unable to compete in the open job market. They include Adult Training Centres, run by local authorities especially for people with learning difficulties, and Sheltered Workshops, run by local authorities or voluntary organisations. Consideration should be given to sub-contracting work to these establishments. Another possibility is to locate people with disabilities who work from home and farm out work to them.

More on mental distress

Although some of what has been said in this chapter applies to people who have experienced mental distress, there are also some issues which are specific to this group and do not apply to people with a physical disability or learning difficulties.

Most people who have been in mental hospital, or psychiatric outpatients, do not think of themselves as having had a disability. They will not think that a reference in a job advertisement to applications from people with disabilities being welcome refers to them. An additional phrase such as 'users and ex-users of mental health services' or 'recipients of psychiatric services' should be included.

If an existing employee is suffering from mental distress which is affecting her or his ability to work, every effort should be made to find out if working conditions have played a part in causing it. It may be that the worker is being sexually harassed, or is feeling the strain of covering up a gay or lesbian lifestyle because s/he does not feel safe to 'come out' at work. S/he may not be receiving adequate supervision or support in her or his work. If there is a problem of this sort, then dealing with it will remove the cause of the distress and make it easier for the worker to be fully effective again.

6

EQUAL OPPORTUNITIES
FOR ALL

The previous three chapters have looked at equal opportunities as they concern groups for whom there is some sort of protective legislation (though in the case of people with disabilities the law is not enforced.) There are other groups which face discrimination: lesbians and gay men find that the law actually sanctions discrimination against them, and working class people are also at a disadvantage in the job market compared with people from other class backgrounds. Both these groups are given space here.

However, that is not where discrimination ends, or where employers should stop thinking about equal opportunities and positive action. Unemployment is especially high among young people. Employers could consider which jobs in their organisation are suitable for school leavers and try and recruit someone suitable from the dole queue. Former offenders, drug addicts and alcoholics all face a similar problem to ex-mental patients. Do they try and cover up their pasts or 'come clean' and take the risk of being unfairly rejected? Voluntary organisations working with disadvantaged groups should be particularly aware of the value of employing people who have experienced that disadvantage themselves.

LESBIANS AND GAY MEN

It is estimated that there are two and a half million lesbians and gay men in the UK. It is often assumed that the figure is far lower, because many lesbians and gay men do not feel safe to disclose their identity. They face widespread discrimination.

The law offers no protection, and has actually sanctioned discrimination. The Employment Appeal Tribunal, which hears appeals in cases under the Employment Protection Act, has found that it can be fair to dismiss someone simply because they are homosexual. *Gay Workers: Trade Unions and the Law* gives examples of tribunal decisions. (See Recommended Reading at the back of this book.) A survey carried out in London by Lesbians and Gay Employment Rights found that 12 out of 200 gay men interviewed had been sacked from their jobs for being gay. (See Useful Organisations at the back of this book.)

The sexual preferences of gay men sometimes become known when they are found guilty of offences for which there is no equivalent for heterosexuals. One such offence is that of 'gross indecency': having sex in a place which the law defines as public, regardless of whether a member of the public sees anything or could have done. Although it is a minor offence, the consequences of being found guilty can be disastrous. Yet a heterosexual couple could have sex in the same situation and not even be guilty of an offence. Other discriminative laws forbid sexual activity between men if one of them is under 21, or if more than two people are involved.

There is a widely held belief that lesbians and gay men are more likely than heterosexual workers, to seduce or corrupt young people, even though there is no evidence that this occurs. Consequently those working or wanting to work with young people, are particularly likely to face discrimination. Doctors sometimes declare lesbians and gay men who are being considered for such work to be medically unfit.

Employers sometimes claim that they will lose business if they are known to be employing a lesbian or a gay man, and pressure also comes from work colleagues who may refuse to work with lesbians or gay men or, who may make them feel unwelcome. Abuse and harassment can reach such a level that the worker is effectively forced to leave the job. It is often believed that lesbians and gay men suffer from 'character defects' including being untrustworthy or temperamental, making them unsuitable for work.

Situations where it is assumed that everyone is heterosexual, and it does not feel safe to 'come out', are difficult for lesbians and gay men. They get a reputation for being a 'bit odd' or secretive because they do not discuss their personal lives, and may have emotional problems arising from the stresses of leading a double life. All these difficulties can affect work performance.

Because they are less likely than most to conform to a 'sexist stereotype', in terms of domestic arrangements, appearance and manner, lesbians are particulary likely to be a target for sexism.

Fear and ignorance about AIDS (Acquired Immune Deficiency Syndrome) has lead to further discrimination against gay men at work. AIDS can be contracted by anyone, regardless of their sexuality. In Britain it is currently mainly gay men who are affected. AIDS is only passed on through body fluids. In practice this is most likely through sexual intercourse or drug users sharing syringes. People may, in this way become infected by the virus HIV, with some going on to develop AIDS or a related illness. It cannot be passed on through normal contact in the workplace and there is no rational reason to refuse to employ or work with gay men, even if they have been found to be likely carriers of the HIV virus.

'AIDS hysteria' has considerably worsened the situation of gay men, who are subjected to more abuse and physical attacks and are more likely to be sacked from work. Even lesbians have been targets, although they are a particularly low risk group.

This shows how 'AIDS hysteria' is based on ignorance, prejudice and fear rather than the real facts about AIDS.

This ignorance, prejudice and fear is being further fuelled by Section 2 [a] in the Local Government Act 1988. It may eventually result in cuts in funding, and the closure of voluntary organisations offering counselling, advice and other services to lesbians and gay men.

Action by employers

The following is a proposal for how the issue can be addressed in an Equal Opportunities Policy Statement of Intent:

'This organisation is opposed to discrimination against lesbians and gay men, and to the notion that they are unsuited to any area of work on grounds of their sexual orientation. We further recognise the right of lesbian and gay staff to be open about their sexuality and will provide adequate redress for those employees who are harassed because of their sexuality'. (From a paper on equal opportunities, positive action and women, given to a conference on 'Women in the Voluntary Sector' organised by the National Council for Civil Liberties and the Association for Clerical, Technical and Supervisory Staff, 1984.)

Added to this could be a statement that discrimination against people who may have the virus HIV, or have AIDS or a related illness, including a refusal to work with them, will be a disciplinary offence.

A programme to put this policy into action could include the following measures:

1 Making it clear in job advertisements that lesbians and gay men are welcome to apply.

2 Avoiding questions about marital status on application forms or at interviews.

3 Informing applicants that when details of criminal records are required, crimes without a heterosexual equivalent will be disregarded.

4 Taking care at interviews not to ask questions about home life which might put pressure on lesbians or gay men to feel they must disclose their identity or lie.

5 Making discrimination or harassment a disciplinary offence and establishing a clear grievance procedure.

6 Leave entitlement which relates to caring for dependants should not discriminate. 'Paternity leave' should become 'child responsibility leave' and be available to any partner of someone who is giving birth. Special leave should also be available to people adopting children. Dependant care leave should not be confined to those caring for family members; other close relationships should be recognised as equally legitimate. (See pages 38 to 42 for more on leave entitlement.)

7 Similarly, pension schemes should allow for payment to dependant partners in the same way as they do for widows.

8 There should be training to make staff aware of 'heterosexism' – the oppression of lesbians and gay men – and 'homophobia' – fear of closeness with people of one's sex – and how they can be overcome. (Homophobia is sometimes used more broadly to mean the fear and loathing of same-sex emotional and sexual relationships.)

WORKING CLASS PEOPLE

Social class can be defined in terms of economic status or culture, or a combination of the two. For the individual, the way they were brought up is likely to be as significant as their current lifestyle when assessing their class position.

It is generally acknowledged that there is a working class, a middle class and an upper class.

The majority of the population is working class. Working class people tend to leave school with few qualifications. Employment is usually low paid with limited opportunity for advancement.

Middle class people have the same relationship to the economy as working class people – as wage earners – and, in that sense are a sub-section of the working class. The difference is that they tend to have higher expectations of success in the education system, and of a career. Work offers more opportunities for taking on greater responsibility, and earning more money, as the person becomes older.

The 'professional' skills required in middle class 'occupations' tend to be more highly valued than the skills required in working class jobs. Compare, say, the social status of a doctor with that of a car mechanic, even though their abilities to recognise symptoms, diagnose the problem and effect a cure are quite comparable.

The status of upper class people usually differs in two respects from that of middle or working class people. Their income is probably mostly from inherited wealth, investments and ownership of companies. They may also have influential positions in industry, financial institutions and politics.

The class system is highly complex. Take, for example, the position of a working class man who starts his own business and is eventually able to live off his investments; or the upper class university student who has a 'nervous breakdown' and ends up in a Salvation Army hostel. The class system also changes. Recent years have seen, on the one hand, a decline in traditional, male working class jobs in heavy industry; and on the other, many more people owning shares.

In Britain — more than in most other countries — there are vast cultural differences between people of different classes. These include differences in political views and values, in accent and use of language, and in ways of relating to other people. People may change their class position in relation to the economic system, but be slower to change in other ways. Because of the importance of culture in determining social class, people who were not born in Britain, or do not regard themselves as part of the mainstream culture, may feel that they do not have a position within the class system.

Because of the complexity of the class system, the way it develops and changes and the way people's position within it can change, some people claim that 'we live in a meritocracy' or that 'class is no longer an issue'.

Yet working class children are at a disadvantage in the educational system. Researchers classify schoolchildren according to their parent's (usually the father's) occupation; ranging from 'professional and managerial' at the top, to 'unskillled' at the bottom. Survey results consistently show that children from the top groups do better than those from the bottom. A number of causes can be identified:

1 Working class children often reject school and all it stands for.

2 Low expectations — they are not expected to do well and so they do not.

3 There is pressure from peers not to do well and stand out from the crowd.

4 The mode of assessment is biased in favour of middle and upper class children.

5 Schools in working class neighbourhoods often have fewer staff and resources, and there is less pressure from parents to raise standards.

6 Middle and upper class children have other material advantages, such as access to private schools — with lower pupil/staff ratios — and bigger houses, where it is easier to find the space to do homework.

7 Working class children often cannot stay in the education system because their families need them to be earning money.

Within the voluntary sector, jobs range from unskilled to professional and managerial. Working class people are employed as caretakers, typists and receptionists. But the public face of voluntary organisations tends to be middle class. Jobs which involve creating policy, developing services or offering advice to people, have a middle class status and are often done by people who were brought up as middle class.

The constituency of most voluntary organisations, however, is working class, because most people are working class and also because many voluntary organisations offer services to the most economically deprived sector of the community.

The situation of middle class workers offering services to working class people can cause problems. If middle class people feel that their values are better than those of working class people, they may try to impose them on people who are using the services provided by their organisation. One example the author has come across is of a working class woman going to an advice agency for help with financial problems, and being lectured on why it is wrong to fiddle social security by someone who would clearly never need to go near the DHSS in her life. There can be some advantages in employing people who share similar values, and have had similar experiences to the people they are working with. These advantages may outweigh such factors as lack of training or formal qualifications.

Groups of people who face other discrimination are likely to be 'over-represented' in the working class, because they are denied access to middle and upper class privileges. This particularly applies to Black people, because the whole family is affected by discrimination. It is striking how Black organisations, when criticising the voluntary sector tend to refer to it being white and middle class. EOPPs for Black people have to take account of this double disadvantage if they are to succeed.

Action by employers

There is no legislation to protect working class people from discrimination. But there is a positive side to this. Employers wanting to offer more opportunities to women and Black people are restricted by legislation. In most cases they must show that they are not discriminating, directly or indirectly, against men or white people. Employers are not restricted in this way when offering opportunities to working class people. A working class background or lifestyle can be an advantage for people doing certain jobs. Employers are free to take account of this in recruitment, training and promotion of workers.

These are some steps which voluntary organisations can take to offer greater equality of opportunity to working class people:

1 Advertise jobs in places where working class people will read them, such as local papers. Avoid the use of jargon, such as 'programme development' when describing jobs. Describe what the person is expected to do, rather than the concept of the job. Avoid mysterious pay scales, such as 'PO 1'. Spell out how much the person doing the job will earn.

2 As has been mentioned elsewhere, the requirement of educational qualifications should be kept to the absolute minimum, and 'life experience' should be valued. This should be made clear in advertisements.

3 Working class people should be mentioned in the organisation's Equal Opportunities Policy Statement of Intent, and given encouragement to apply for jobs, in advertisements.

4 Working class employees should be encouraged to go on training courses and apply for promotion.

5 People who interview job applicants should be trained to become aware of the possibilty of having an unconscious bias towards those with similar life experiences to themselves. These may be indicated by accent, dress and manner,as well as in more direct ways, such as having been to the same university.

6 Classism awareness training should be developed for all people involved in the organisation. The voluntary sector is only just beginning to address class issues and will make significant strides forward when greater clarity has been achieved. This can only come about through workers taking time to think about and discuss their own class backgrounds and prejudices, in the same way that they tackle issues such as sexism and racism.

7

The wider picture

So far this guide has focused on equal opportunites in relation to employment. But there are other issues which are also worthy of attention. The selection of volunteers and members of management committees can raise similar issues to those which voluntary organisations face as employers. Many voluntary agencies sponsor government training schemes, and the recruitment and treatment of trainees is an equal opportunities issue. Organisations wishing to attract members will be more effective if they can derive support from all sectors of the community. An organisation's policies will reflect the unconscious oppressive attitudes of its decision-makers unless strong action is taken to prevent it.

An EOPP needs to take all these issues into account. The success of one part is, to some extent, dependent on the others. Positive action to recruit more women to senior positions will stand a greater chance of success if it is part of a package of measures the organisation is taking to become more responsive to issues which affect women.

■ People from all walks of life do voluntary unpaid work. A national survey found that the proportion of women and men is about the same. Upper and middle class people tend to do voluntary work more than working class people. It is not clear what proportion of volunteers are from ethnic communities or have a disability, but these people face discrimination in voluntary activity just as they do in employment. A worker with a volunteer placement agency described a way that racism is perpetuated. 'We have people who will say things like "I don't think he'd be happy here because he'd be the only Black person".' People with disabilities are denied opportunities to do voluntary work because there is not the right physical

VOLUNTEERS

provision for their needs (e.g. wheelchair access) or because no-one has thought through what needs to be done to overcome any initial difficulties.

Voluntary work can be a route into employment as it gives people the opportunity to gain useful experience. Indeed many organisations regularly recruit staff from their volunteers. This can be a way of making an EOPP in employment effective – providing opportunities to people who have been denied access to suitable education and work experience elsewhere.

It is important then that an organisation's volunteers policy is one which is fair to all and does not become exploitative in any way. These are some steps which can be taken to make it that way:

1 Incorporate a statement about volunteers in your Equal Opportunities Policy Statement of Intent.

2 Inform places from which you recruit volunteers that you welcome volunteers from ethnic communities, and with disabilities etc.

3 If advertising for volunteers, do so in places where they are likely to be seen by people from all sections of the community.

4 Make sure that people responsible for recruiting and supervising volunteers have done awareness training.

5 Monitor the results of your volunteers policy and consider them at your annual review.

Community Service Volunteers can be a good source of volunteers from groups which face discrimination. It accepts anyone between the age of 16 and 35 and places them in projects involving contact with people. It has particular experience of working out suitable arrangements for people with disabilities. (See Useful Organisations at the back of this book.)

MANAGEMENT COMMITTEES

Also included here are trustees of charities and directors of limited companies, and any governing body of a voluntary organisation. The people in these bodies tend to either have professional skills which are useful to the organisation or have useful contacts. This generally means occupying a postion of power (e.g. being a local councillor or the chair of a body such as the Chamber of Commerce). Discrimination tends to mean that people with these skills or in these positions are white, male, middle class, able-bodied and heterosexual. 94 per cent of MPs are men, and the 1981 census showed that 89 per cent of chartered and certified accountants and 84 per cent of university academic staff are also male.

It is not surprising then, that a survey of Councils for Voluntary Service found that although 69 per cent of staff were women, only 38 per cent of the members of main committees were female.

To have a management committee made up of people from similarly privileged backgrounds can cause all sorts of problems. Because the way society is organised has benefitted them, they may find it difficult to accept that there is anything wrong, and resist progressive policies, including EOPPs. They may have a blinkered attitude to trade unions and try to stop staff from joining them, finding it hard to understand the needs and aspirations of women, people from ethnic communities and working class people.

Voluntary organisations wanting to change the composition of their management committees may find themselves hindered by constitutional requirements (e.g. that there should be two councillors on the committee) and practical considerations – contacts and professional skills are useful. Nevertheless, changes can be made, but to attract sufficient numbers of suitable people who are representative of the organisation's constituency, it is probably necessary to break down the usual 'management committee-worker-volunteer-client' hierarchy.

Here is an example of how a mental health day centre has done that successfully, described by one of the workers:

'We see our role as promoting mental health in the community. We try and respond to the needs of the users as they perceive them. By users I mean people who come to the centre for therapy or to attend classes and workshops; those who come to help out, and people leading activities here. Often these are the same people. We do not distinguish between clients and volunteers. We have had a users' committee for some time. It was consulted but did not make important decisions. Now most of the management committee is elected by and from the users' group. The other members are either officers (such as the treasurer and secretary) or co-opted because the constitution requires it (local councillors, someone from social services etc). There was some concern expressed by the old management committee that there would be difficulties arising from the situation where someone who is the client of a paid worker and also their boss, but it's worked out fine in practice. In fact the meetings are much better now. I used to go away feeling drained. The emphasis has changed. People are not trying to impress anybody. They know what is going on in the centre. The more control people have over their lives the healthier they are. It is a fundamental right. Many mental health services rob people of that power.'

■   Voluntary organisations often act as agents or sponsors for training schemes, such as the Adult Training Programme and Youth Training Scheme (YTS). Much of what has been said about recruitment and training for employees will apply to participants on these schemes.

For people on YTS it will be their first work experience, which puts a particular onus on those running the schemes to treat them equally and help them overcome the effects of past discrimination in the education system. This might involve, for example, encouraging young women to acquire skills in non-traditional work areas. All supervisors on

**PARTICIPANTS
IN GOVERNME[]
TRAINING
SCHEMES**

such schemes can benefit from awareness training, as can the trainees themselves.

■ Most voluntary organisations are either offering a service or trying to change things. Some do both. All will be more effective if they take into account the needs and views of all sections of the community.

Take, for example, an organisation offering an advice service in a multi-racial area. If it is seen as being a white organisation it will probably be under-used by Black people. If the centre is not meeting their needs, they have been deprived of a service they are entitled to. The well-intentioned staff and management committee may well protest that Black people are welcome to use their services and will be treated fairly, but if that message has not been successfully put across, the organisation is not being effective.

A good first step would be to recruit Black people to the staff and management committee. Special projects aimed at meeting the particular needs of ethnic communities could be set up: these could include a project to explain their right to welfare benefits to people whose first language is not English, or expert advice on immigration issues. Keeping records of who is using the centre will show if the new policy is being successful.

Pressure groups trying to change government policy will want to involve as many people as possible in their activities from all sections of the community. A group concerned with conservation may find that public opinion polls show that the issue is of particular interest to women, but that most of its active supporters are men. Investigations may then suggest that child-care responsibilities are restricting women's involvement. Organising a creche at the annual conference may be a first move, but is not necessarily the best solution for the women and children involved. It also lets local branches off the hook. Persuading branches to organise child-care locally may be difficult, but it will have more effect by enabling more women to join in the group's activities at a local level.

And what about people with disabilities? How about having a sign language interpreter at a national demonstration so that deaf people can understand the announcements and speeches?

The equal opportunities implications of service provision and membership recruitment will be different for each voluntary organisation. If it is already involving people from all sectors of the community, as workers and on its management committee, your organisation will find it easier to establish how it needs to change in this respect.

Special training can educate all staff to be aware of the equal opportunities implications of their work: the publicity officer will remember to have Black faces as well as white on a poster; the conference organiser will think to arrange for someone to monitor the proportion of women and men speaking from the floor and alert the chair if women are being ignored; the adminstrator, looking for new premises, will want to find a building which can be made wheelchair accessible.

Taken one at a time these actions may not appear to be of any great significance, but if enough organisations act in these ways individually it will change the face of voluntary sector activity in this country.

CONCLUSION

It will be clear by now that equal opportunities work takes time, energy and money. The question is how much and is it worth it?

There are direct costs involved in such measures as additional maternity pay and in attending or organising training courses. There is also the cost of staff time involved in drawing up, agreeing and implementing the EOPP and monitoring its progress. This time can be considerable, especially in the early stages. An ambitious and comprehensive programme can cause a great deal of upheaval. It is likely to bring differences in attitude and political belief to the fore. The decision-making processes of the organisation may be tested to the full and found wanting.

If the implementation of an EOPP is seen as a diversion from the 'real' work of the organisation then it will not seem worth it. But this is not a marginal issue. If your organisation is ignoring the needs and concerns of many of the people within its constituency, then it is not doing its job properly. If it is denying employment opportunities to Black people or working class people, however unintentionally, then it is abusing its power and perpetuating oppression. Equal opportunities work is not an additional burden to an organisation but the key to more effective work.

Of course not everything has to be done at once. And small organisations with insecure funding may have, temporarily or periodically, to postpone some aspects of equal opportunity work. But the whole notion of equal opportunities does not have to be abandoned just because progress needs to be slow and piecemeal.

Some people will throw up their hands in horror at all the talk of contracts of employment and conditions of service. But organisations which ignore the welfare of their staff usually run into difficulties eventually. The introduction of dependant care leave does not have to be taken as a sign that the organisation has lost its radical edge and is settling into middle age. It may mean that it can attract more talented staff and not lose them so quickly because of 'burn out'.

Even the arguments – should they occur – may prove to be worthwhile in the long term. Many voluntary organisations feel so desperate to act thay they throw themselves into the fray, without having thoroughly thought out what they are trying to achieve and how they should go about it, or even how they would make such decisions in the first place. If there are underlying tensions, disagreements and conflicts then they will already be adversely affecting the work of the organisation. If, in attempting to agree and implement an EOPP, the organisation is forced to deal with these difficulties that may be all to the good.

Taking on equal opportunities work is a growing experience. It makes people think deeply, about themselves, the organisation and the world around them. It releases energy and creativity. Even if we have not thought about it consciously, we know there is something wrong if everyone in the management committee has been to public school, or Black people don't come on demonstrations, or women stay away from meetings. It is a relief to start putting these things right.

Useful organisations
mentioned in the book

● *Commission for Racial Equality,*
Elliot House, 10-12 Allington St, London SW1E 5EH.
Tel: 01 828 7022.
● *Community Service Volunteers,*
Head Office, 237 Pentonville Rd, London N1 9NJ.
Tel: 01 278 6601.
● *Equal Opportunities Commission,*
Overseas House, Quay St, Manchester M3 3HN.
Tel: 061 833 9244.
● *Lesbian and Gay Employment Rights* (LAGER),
Room 203, Southbank House, Black Prince Road, London SE1 7SJ.
Tel: 01 587 1643.
● *National Council for Civil Liberties,*
21 Tabard St, London SE1 4LA.
Tel: 01 403 3888.
● *National Equivalence Information Centre,*
British Council, 10 Spring Gardens, London SW1A 2BN.
Tel: 01 930 8466.
● *Royal National Institute for the Blind,*
224 Great Portland St, London W1N 6AA.
Tel: 01 388 1266.
● *Royal National Institute for the Deaf,*
105 Gower St, London WC1E 6AH.
Tel: 01 387 8033.
● *Royal Society for Mentally Handicapped Children and Adults* (MENCAP),
National Headquarters, 123 Golden Lane, London EC1Y ORT.
Tel: 01 253 9433.
● *Spastics Society,*
12 Park Crescent, London W1N 4EQ.
Tel: 01 636 5020.
● *Workplace Nurseries Campaign,*
Room 205, Southbank House, Black Prince Road, London SE1 7SJ.
Tel: 01 582 7199.

Recommended reading

CHAPTER TWO

Free publications:

● *Implementing Equal Opportunity Policies*
● *Monitoring an Equal Opportunity Policy*
● Catalogue of other publications

Available from:
Commission for Racial Equality,
Elliott House, 10-12 Allington Street, London SW1E 5EH.
Tel: 01 828 7022.

● *Directory of Race Relations & Equal Opportunities Trainers*

Available from:
Local Government Training Board,
4th Floor, Arndale House, Arndale Centre, Luton LU1 2TS.
Tel: 0582 21166.

● *Discipline at Work. The ACAS Advisory Handbook*

Available from:
Your regional office of the
Advisory, Conciliation and Arbitration Service, or Head Office,
27 Wilton Street, London SW1X 7AZ.
Tel: 01 210 3600.

Publications to buy:

● *A Multi-Racial Society: The Role of National Voluntary Organisations*
Michaela Dungate for NCVO Ethnic Minorities Working Party.
Bedford Square Press. 1984.

Available from:
Bookshops or Harper and Row Distributors Ltd.
Estover Road, Plymouth PL6 7PZ.
Tel: 0752 70525.

● *Equal Opportunity Employment Policies: Guidelines for Voluntary Organisations*
1986.

Available from:
North Kensington Law Centre,
74 Golborne Road, London W10.
Tel: 01 969 7473.

● *A Guide to the Implementation of an Equal Opportunity Policy*
Sheena Dunbar and Larry Ward. MIND S.E. Regional Office. 1987.

Available from:
MIND Mail Order Dept.
4th Floor, 24-32 Stephenson Way, London NW1 2HD.
Tel: 01 387 9126

● *Training: The Implementation of Equal Opportunities at Work*
Vols 1 & 2. CRE. 1988.

Available from:
Commission for Racial Equality,
Elliot House, 10-12 Allington Street, London SW1E 5EH.
Tel: 01 828 7022.

Free publications:

● *Sex discrimination: A guide to the Sex Discrimination Act*
● *Equal Opportunities: A guide for Employers – the Employment Provisions of the Sex Discrimination Act*
● *The Sex Discrimination Act and Advertising: Guidance Notes*
● *So You Think You've Got It Right . . . Further Guidance for Equal Opportunity Employers with Special Reference to Internal Advertising*
● *Equal Pay for Work of Equal Value: A Guide to the Amended Equal Pay Act*
● *A Model Equal Opportunities Policy*
● *Job Evaluation Schemes Free of Sex Bias*
● Catalogue of other publications

CHAPTER THREE

Available from:
Equal Opportunities Commission,
Overseas House, Quay Street, Manchester M3 3HN.
Tel: 061 833 9244.
Enclose an S.A.E. with your order.

● *Pregnant at Work*

Available from:
Maternity Alliance,
15 Britannia Street, London WC1X 9JP.
Tel: 01 837 1265.
Enclose an S.A.E. with your order.

● *Employers Guide to Statutory Maternity Pay* (NI 257) DHSS

Available from:
Local Social Security Offices or DHSS Leaflets,
P O Box 21, Stanmore, Middlesex HA7 1AY.

Publications to buy:

● *Maternity Rights at Work*
Jean Coussins, Lyn Durward and Ruth Evans. NCCL. 1987.
● *Part-time Workers Need Full-time Rights.*
Ann Sedley. NCCL. 1983.
● *Positive Action: Changing the Workplace for Women.*
Paddy Stamp and Sadie Robarts. NCCL. 1986.
● *Sexual Harassment at Work.*
Ann Sedley and Melissa Benn. NCCL. 1982.

Available from:
National Council for Civil Liberties,
21 Tabard Street, London SE1 4LA.
Tel: 01 403 3888.

● *Job Sharing and Voluntary Organisations*
NCVO. 1983.

Available from:
National Council for Voluntary Organisations,
26 Bedford Square, London WC1B 3HU.
Tel: 01 636 4066.
or
New Ways to Work,
309 Upper Street, London N1 2TY.
Tel: 01 226 4026.

● *The Position of Women within Councils for Voluntary Service*
Eve Hay. National Association of CVS. 1985.

Available from:
National Association of Councils for Voluntary Service,
26 Bedford Square, London WC1B 3HU.
Tel: 01 636 4066.

Free publications:

● *List of Ethnic Minority Press*
● *Sharp Calendar of Religious Festivals*
● *Religious Observance by Muslim Employees: A framework for discussion*
● *Race Relations Code of Practice*
● *Race Discrimination: A guide to the Race Relations Act, 1976*
● *A Guide to the Race Relations Act, 1976: Advertising*
● *Guidelines for Advertisers and Publishers. Race Relations Act, 1976:
Employment Advertisements*
● Catalogue of other publications

Available from:
Commission for Racial Equality,
10-12 Allington Street, London SW1E 5EH.
Tel: 01 828 7022.

● *Equal Opportunities: Some steps towards Race Equality in Employment*

Available from:
Southwark Council for Voluntary Service,
135 Rye Lane, London SE15.
Tel: 01 732 3731.

Publications to buy:

● *'We want to be anti-racist . . . but we don't know what to do' A Study of
anti-racist practice in London's Voluntary Sector.*
LVCS. 1986.

Available from:
London Voluntary Service Council,
68 Charlton Street, London NW1 1JR.
Tel: 01 388 0241.

Free publications:

● *Code of Good Practice in the Employment of Disabled People*
● *Employing Someone with . . .* Series of Leaflets covering Deafness, Epilepsy, Haemophilia, Blindness, Multiple Sclerosis, 'Mental Illness' and 'Mental Handicap'.

Available from:
Disablement Advisory Service.
Contact through your local Department of Employment office.

79

RECOMMENDED
READING

Publications to buy:

● *Sickle Cell Disease: A guide for families*
Elizabeth N Anionwu and Harun B Jibril. 1986.

Available from:
Sickle Cell Society,
Green Lodge, Barretts Green Road, London NW10 7AP.
Tel: 01 961 7795/8346.

● *Employer's Guide to Disabilities*
Melvyn Kettle and Bert Massie. 1987.

Available from:
Royal Association for Disability and Rehabilitation,
25 Mortimer Street, London W1N 8AB.
Tel: 01 637 5400.

● *A Right to Work: Disability and Employment*
Susan Lonsdale and Alan Walker. 1984.

Available from:
Low Pay Unit,
9 Poland Street, London W1V 3DG.
Tel: 01 437 1780.
or
Disability Alliance,
25 Denmark Street, London WC2 8NJ.
Tel: 01 240 0806.

● *Factsheets about mental distress.* A series produced by MIND.

Available from:
MIND Mail Order Dept.
24-32 Stephenson Way, London NW1 2HD.
Tel: 01 387 9126.

CHAPTER SIX

80

Free publications:

● *AIDS and Employment*

Available from:
Dept. of Employment and the Health and Safety Executive,
The Mailing House, Leeland Road, London W13 9HL.

● *Danger! Heterosexism at Work: A Handbook on Equal Opportunities in the Workplace for Lesbians and Gay Men*

Available from:
ALA, 36 Old Queen Street, London SW1.
Tel: 01 222 7799.

Publications to buy:

● *Gay Workers: Trade Unions and the Law*
Chris Bear, Roland Jeffrey and Terry Munyard. NCCL. 1983.

Available from:
National Council for Civil Liberties,
21 Tabard Street, London SE1 4LA.
Tel: 01 403 3888.

● *Gay Men at Work*
Phil Greasley. LAGER. 1986.

Available from:
Lesbian and Gay Employment Rights,
Room 203, Southbank House, Black Prince Road, London SE1 7SJ.
Tel: 01 587 1643.

Printed by Spider Web, 14-16 Sussex Way, London N7 6RS

Cover Design – Gill Johns and Roger Huddle
Book Design – Roger Huddle
Typesetting – Artworkers Typesetters, London EC1V 4NJ. 01-833 0425
Print Production – Anderson Fraser, 230-232 Holloway Road,
London N7 8DA. 01-607 8811